Journeys

by

Alan Forman

JOURNEYS

by

Alan Forman

First published 2005

ISBN 0-9551056-0-9

Cover design by Alan Forman, artwork by Malcolm Henwood
Internal design and layout by the Alpha Xperience, Newbury, Berkshire.
Printed and bound by the Alpha Xperience, Newbury, Berkshire.

Published by Janathel Publishing,
Aysgarth, Whitehill Road,
Meopham, Kent DA13 0NZ
Email: acform@btinternet.com

From where copies of this book may be obtained

Alan Forman spent most of his working life in telecommunications as an engineer, and then as a manager. As an engineer he went up the poles, down the holes and mended telephone exchanges. As a manager he was involved with staff control at several levels.

He worked with the Samaritans for several years and was involved in Christian youth work. He served as a deacon in the Baptist church and is trying very hard to be an Anglican at present, but in reality is just a simple Christian!

He has been involved with counselling for over fifteen years working as a redeployment counsellor with BT, in a G.P. practice and within a hospice setting. He is currently a counsellor with Sevenoaks Christian Counselling Service, where he also works as an affiliate for an international employee assistance programme, whose clients come from within local commerce and industry.

He is married to Carolyn, lives in the village of Meopham in Kent and has three children and three grandchildren.

This book is about a counsellor's journey on a bicycle from Land's End to John O'Groats. Along the way he stops off and takes a look at many of the places and issues he and his clients have encountered on their journeys.

July 2005

This book is dedicated to James, Nathan and Eleanor

whose journeys have just begun.

Acknowledgements

Thanks to all the clients who have enriched my life

as I have travelled with them up and down the hills of their journeys.

To my friends Christine, Stephen and Jean

who read and checked my manuscript.

All the client stories described in this book are based on actual events but to ensure complete confidentiality the author has used them in a way that will protect his clients.

Contents

Physiology of Journeys

Some other milestones on life's journey

Depression

Abuse

The end of the journey is in sight

Journeys

Prologue

The Beginning of The Road

Why did I want to cycle 1000 plus miles? I've never been a *real cyclist* – never been in a cycling club or done time trials. My very earliest memory of riding a bike was about age five, on a tricycle at home in Erith. I seem to recall that it was run over by the milkman with his horse and cart. I don't remember if I was on it at the time but because I have no enduring fear of horses or dislike of milk, I suspect that I wasn't!

I know that my Dad was a cyclist and did some racing at Herne Hill and was in a cycle club, but this was long before I was around. He was also a good athlete and enjoyed most ball games.

My mother, now in her 80s, was, and still is, very skilled with a racket and a golf club, but not usually at the same time and only in our back garden these days. It is interesting to see that our eldest grandchild, James, is also very sporting, and needs no encouragement to kick, throw or hit a ball and it is usually embraced in some competitive way, that almost always guarantees him a win!

I never played football at Wembley, cricket at Lords, golf at St Andrews or tennis at Wimbledon. If you have ever seen me play snooker then you'll know why I've never played at the Crucible. I haven't canoed across the English Channel or climbed Mount Everest so there wasn't much else left on the sporting stage to have a go at.

This small book is about my thoughts on the psychology, spirituality and physiology of my journey. I have tried to embrace some of the most common issues that have surfaced during my 15 years as a counsellor and attempted to entwine those with my limited understanding of riding a bike.

My earliest memories of competitive sport were junior school days. I played a lot with a boy who lived close by and who was to become a legend on our country's sporting stage. Alan Knott, although a year younger than me, was so good at cricket and football that he played in my year group and was still the best player in the team. He went on to play cricket for Kent and England and became, arguably, the best wicket-keeper batsman of all time.

In my training for the Counselling Diploma, which I studied as part of my redundancy package from B.T., I looked at the issues around nature and nurture and believe that, to a large extent, we are products of both. However the idea that we are programmed by our genetic map to follow a set path is a denial of personal choice and the effects of our environment. Comparing identical and non-identical twins, along with adoption studies have shown that genetics play a considerable roll in determining many, but not all of our characteristics. These handed down genes create a *predisposing towards* certain conditions. It is thought that it is our environment, which includes our time in the womb from conception, and continues through our nurturing, also affects our brain as it is developing. So in a way it comes as little surprise that because of my genetic map and my upbringing that I have a sporting tendency and that may go some way to explaining the *why cycle 1000 miles* question.

Choices

In supporting the notion of nature *and* nurture I would say most forcefully that we have personal responsibility and choices as well. If you ever doubt this philosophy then read the great little book written by Victor Frankl, *Man's Search for Meaning*. Here the author, a Jew in a Nazi death camp, and having seen most of his family exterminated, describes the choices he had, even when stripped naked and in line for the gas chamber himself. How could he, every possession lost, every value destroyed, and suffering from hunger, cold and brutality, still find meaning and purpose in living? Having read Frankl's story you can never again claim you can't have responsibility for your actions or the chance to choose.

If Frankl had choices in that most dire of circumstances then a good case can be made to suggest that we also have to accept some personal responsibility for our own lives and actions whilst not denying the influences of the past.

Although Victor Frankl died several years ago I am sure he would chuckle at a paper presented by a Professor Schwartz to the Royal Society of Arts in London. He talked about *choice fatigue* and how our happiness is threatened by *too much* choice. He says that we now have 20 different styles of jeans to choose from, 24 flavours of jam, 38 types of breakfast cereal and 22 models of mobile phones. Schwartz suggests that given such an array of choice we often end up doing nothing.

If you are thinking of buying a bike please don't go into your local cycle centre and say. 'Excuse me I want to buy a bike.' The assistant might laugh just a little. Do you want a racer or tourer, a steel aluminium or carbon fibre frame; an A.T.B. (all terrain bike) a recumbent, a fold up, a hybrid? And so it goes on!!

Perhaps the 20th century psychologist Maslow puts his finger on another reason *why ride a thousand miles* in his Theory of Human Motivation. In his hierarchy of needs, sometimes known as the Maslovian triangle, see appendix 1, one of the stages that builds towards what Maslow describes as self-actualisation, is the need for achieving one's full potential – a sign that we must do what we can do.

Jung, the Swiss psychiatrist, also perceived human growth as a gradual process, a bit like the imprint of a giant oak tree within the tiny acorn. For people of faith this might be the fulfilling of the image within them implanted by their creator, and this of course is not just about riding a bike a long way, but the emergence of an individual made in the image of that creator.

I would argue with the writer John Keble in the hymn *New Every Morning* that 'the trivial round, the common task will furnish all we need to ask'. I don't believe that for one moment – I get very bored with the mundane; I believe we need to be stimulated and challenged. There are, of course, people for whom routine and order are a vital necessity, the very young and very old are examples of this, but caged animals in some zoos show distress despite having their basic needs met. We hear children saying, 'I'm bored.' For them especially challenge, stimulation, excitement and even fear is important for a rounded personality to emerge.

When Carolyn was running a Home for the elderly it was great to see how she and her partner broke the stereotypical mould of people of sitting around the edge of a room staring into open space. They provided physical, intellectual and spiritual stimulus on a daily basis and people even in their 90s responded positively.

As a schoolboy I can remember a visit to the Ford factory in Dagenham where men really did sit and put hub caps on the Cortina or the Capri or was it the Anglia? Anyway the unions eventually won the day and team building was introduced on the production line to try and minimise boredom and give the workers some sense of pride. These days cars are built by computers, but no more at Dagenham. That's progress I suppose!

It would seem that the present day industrial revolution with the growth of call centres is rediscovering the problems of the mid 20th century with high absenteeism and rapid staff turnover. These statistics seem to be linked to the same psychological problems that were the basis of the strife experienced by the workers of 50 years ago.

My earliest memories evoking wonder and not a little fear would have been the Eagle comic, Enid Blyton's Famous Five, Children's Hour on the Home Service and Journey into Space also on the radio. I still reckon you get a better picture listening to the radio or reading a good book than from a slim, flat, wide screen, plasma, wrap around, nicam, pro-logic, digital television. I remember my sister hiding behind the settee when Dr Who came on T.V. ... and that was just the theme music! The challenges for me continued throughout schooling and in The Boys' Brigade. I was always competitive if not combative.

So why did I do the ride? I had a choice, nobody forced me to ride from Land's End to John O' Groats, *end to end* as it is called. I exercised my free will, definitely not free wheel!

My understanding therefore is that we all have choices about our lives and they are made in the knowledge that a cocktail of factors influences our decisions.

If you have been incubating a wish why not cancel your subscription to the procrastination society, get out there and do it!

So *achieving potential* ...as Maslow puts it, does seem to fit. I've wanted to test myself on some recognised ultimate test and Land's End to John O' Groats had been at the back of my mind for some time.

The Bikes and When The Wheels First Started Turning

My first real bike, after the squashed tricycle, was a Rudge, 14 inch wheel with a 3-speed Sturmey Archer gear. My Dad bought me this after I passed the 11 plus and was offered a place at Erith Technical School. I knew it was a second-hand bike but it was my pride and joy and the chrome used to gleam. It's funny how bikes always seem to go faster and smoother when they are clean. This was the bike on which I did nearly all my early riding, but only to the shops, school and church.

I remember my Grandmother and Grandad, who lived at Bearsted, near Maidstone, having an old bone-shaker of a bike. My sister and I used to ride up and down their lane; it was an unadopted, unmade farm track with loads of potholes and a railway bridge at the end, which produced an echo when you stood underneath it and shouted.

I love the way Lance Armstrong, now seven times winner of the Tour de France, describes what it is about a child's first bike. He says, 'It is the long-sought means of transportation for all of us who have runaway hearts. Our first bike is a matter of kerb-jumping, puddle-splashing liberation; it's freedom from supervision, from car-pools and curfews. It's a merciful release from reliance on parents, one's own way to the movies or a friend's house. More plainly, it's the first chance we have to choose our own direction.' I can relate to all of that, if only it were true for the children of today in our land!

When I started work as an apprentice at Fraser and Chalmers in Erith, and earned some money, I bought the Holdsworth cycle, which I still have today. It, too, was second-hand, but had Campagnolo gears, a sort of holy kit in the 1960s. I would have used it for my *end to end* but spares are becoming difficult to obtain. Everything on it is measured in inches and all the bits in the bike shops today seem to be measured in centimetres, whatever they are!

I bought my first ever new bike in 2002 with the *end to end* in mind. It was a Trek 1200 with an aluminium frame. (Full specification in appendix 2.) It was a lot lighter than my old Holdsworth and a totally different gearing system which took a lot of getting used to after 40 years on the Holdsworth. During the 1980s I had bought another bike; this was, strangely enough, another Rudge, but a mountain bike and is mainly used off road.

On my *end to end* I took with me a Moulton AM7 with a three speed Sturmey Archer gear. This is a small-wheeled bike using a multitubular space frame and has front and rear suspension. Although very old, it's great fun to ride but a lot harder work than the Trek. The Moulton was a spare for me in case of serious breakdown of the Trek. Carolyn also likes riding it and she used it a few times to visit local shops from the campsites as well as visiting distant loos on some sites!

The Charities

After the decision was made to attempt the journey I felt I wanted to ride for some good causes and the choice of charities was not difficult. Appendix 3 gives final amounts raised.

Cancer Research U.K. is the organisation whose research into cancer gave my sister Sue hope after being diagnosed with multiple myeloma. Very few members of our family have had cancer-related illnesses not connected to lifestyle, so quite where this came from, at such a relatively young age, remains a mystery. My sister has worked tirelessly for the organisation since her recovery.

The Ellenor Foundation is a charity working in North Kent, providing hospice care for patients with life-threatening diseases who wish to remain in their own homes. The care that patients receive is free of charge to them. Carolyn has worked in various positions for this great organisation for the past five years.

Sevenoaks Christian Counselling Service (S.C.C.S) is a charity providing one-to-one counselling for people struggling with marital, emotional, psychological, spiritual and work-related concerns. Many of their clients are unable to pay the full cost of their counselling. S.C.C.S were bold enough to welcome me into their team over six years ago.

St. John's Church Meopham is at the heart of our village and has become our spiritual home. Carolyn and I are both actively involved in the work and worship at St. John's and are trying to be Anglicans despite our Baptist roots.

I've never been very good at asking people for money and so I wasn't too sure who to ask about sponsorship; I feel that we are constantly bombarded with good causes that need support. I decided to write to all the people on our Christmas card list as well as the people associated with S.C.C.S and St. John's Church. We were both amazed at the response with nearly 200 individual sponsors and publicity in local newspapers and the Parish Magazine. We stopped collecting at the end of August 2003 and 99 per cent of sponsors had responded.

Mainly through the efforts of our daughter Judith, ably assisted by our other daughter Emma, nearly all the sponsors were contacted a couple of weeks after I'd completed the ride, and over 100 people turned up at our house for a surprise get-together. I had absolutely no idea this was going to happen. There were relatives, friends from my B.T. life, colleagues from S.C.C.S., life long acquaintances, neighbours and members from St. John's and Emmanuel Baptist Church, Gravesend. They all brought a bottle and plate of something; everyone had their fill, the sun shone and a great time was had by all. A truly amazing evening.

Constraints, Or Why I Should Not Have Attempted The Ride

My knees have little or no cartilage left in them caused mainly by football injuries and numerous operations, so standing up on the pedals like real cyclists do, when hill climbing, is not an option. I have to rely on thigh power because I cannot transfer body weight through my knee joints without considerable pain and subsequent swelling. Which is of course why walking around Sainsbury's or Safeway or Bluewater, even for a few minutes, is no-go territory! Walking on grass with a set of golf clubs is of course far easier!! Only a couple of months after the ride my left knee developed a Baker's cyst which ruptured and left me unable to walk, let alone ride, so perhaps my fears about my dodgy knees were justified. Or was it the ride that caused the problem – who knows?

Food For The Ride

I was given dried and semi-dried fruit by Nicci, a colleague at work, and Kendal Mint Cake from my daughter Judith and Dr Andrew from the Ellenor Foundation. I ate cereals, bread with honey and fruit juice for breakfast. Carolyn made me thick sandwiches of peanut butter, cheese and pickle, and I carried two litres of orange squash on my bike, along with portions of dried fruit and mint cake. I enjoyed a piece of homemade flapjack almost every day immediately after the ride, washed down with a mug of tea. After meeting up with Emma and her husband Richard at Shrewsbury, I carried a different drink. Emma brought me a case of Coca-Cola's latest sports drink – she was working for the company at the time. I didn't like the flavour much but it was supposed to do you good. It contained some fast-acting carbohydrates, minerals and electrolytes designed to delay the onset of muscle fatigue during exercise.

Dr Andrew, who does some biking himself, visited me before the ride. He explained the chemistry of food science to me. I really had no idea how important eating the correct foods were for endurance events. My friend Colin ended up in hospital after running the London marathon a couple of months before my ride, despite eating and drinking what he thought was the right food. Apparently he was on the wrong sort of fluid! I was very grateful for all the advice given and apart from losing about 14 lbs. in weight, suffered no obvious side effects.

Strategy For Riding -or Did I Make It Up as I went Along?

I reviewed several books that focused on the *end to end* ride. *The Cyclists Touring Club (C.T.C.)* issue several schedules. *The Lonely Planet Guide on Cycling in Great Britain* also covers the route in some detail, but I settled on *Bike Britain* by Paul Salter. It gives excellent detail and breaks the ride down into 21 days, mainly on B roads, which was about the schedule I wanted. In fact I managed to compress the ride down to 20 days; there did seem to be a certain symmetry in 1000 miles in 20 days. My mind produced that bit of logic without asking my legs!!

Each day's riding was detailed in the book in the form of a map that showed all the significant climbs and places of interest en route along with photographs. It felt at times that, far from giving signposts along the way, the author was almost allowing me to follow his footprints. He had obviously made the journey himself.

As long as I did not get lost, the maps were great but when I did get lost they were not of sufficient detail to get me back on the right trail.

Lots of people asked why I went from south to north. I wish I had a pound for my charities from all the people who told me it was uphill going that way! The reason for my choice was because of the prevailing wind, this is predominately from the south or southwest during the summer months.

We chose the month of June because it was outside school holidays and the days gave us plenty of daylight. The risk was that it could have been too hot. It was on some days, but the further north we travelled the cooler it got.

Training

I had a medical in January, just to make sure that nothing too obvious was going on that I didn't know about – but that didn't include a brain scan! I think I passed and went into serious – well, serious for me ! – training just after that.

I used a 20 mile round trip from Meopham to Dartford and back via Wrotham. This gave me some speed training – speed of course is a relative term – along flat roads on the outward journey and hill climbing on the return.

I built up to a distance of about 100 miles a week by the middle of May, and also did a couple of 50 mile rides. I was swimming once a week and built up slowly towards a distance of about a mile in a session. My knees were a constant source of concern, but only a couple of times did they swell enough to restrict training.

The bike behaved quite well during the training runs. I had several punctures, which was fine because it gave me a chance to test my tool kit. Only twice did I have to return the Trek to the shop. The bottom bracket bearing came loose; I certainly did not want that problem on the ride, although I did carry the tools for such repairs in the camper van. The other training breakdown occurred on the first ride with the Trek.

A jockey wheel fell out of the gear mechanism. I had to walk home. The bike shop denied all responsibility and blamed it on the man in Taiwan who assembled – or in this case, failed to assemble it. When I pointed out that the pre-delivery inspection carried out by the shop included a tick in a box for 'check gear mech' they muttered something along the lines of, 'You just can't get staff these days.'

Daily Riding Routine

I knew I had to try to complete the first 10 miles each day without stopping, in order to get my knees going – because I knew from training that they were always quite painful for some time until they had warmed up – or whatever knees do! I had been given some Emu Oil to rub in; this was from Rita, a neighbour who attends St. John's. She did offer to accompany me on the ride and apply the magic liniment personally, but I had to decline her generous offer. However Carolyn did a great job as a masseuse every night. I continued to take glucosamine and cod liver oil tablets, which had been prescribed by friends who have knowledge of such things. I'm not entirely convinced about the efficacy of such chemicals but they seemed to do no harm.

I carried a compass, so if all else failed with my navigation, at least I'd be able to head north. Most of the ride was on B roads so I did expect to get lost a few times. I carried a spare inner tube and a puncture repair kit on the bike in case I was unlucky enough to get two punctures in one day. I also had a mobile phone but kept it switched off.

I had a spare tyre in the camper van along with spokes, a chain and brake blocks. A comprehensive tool kit including bottom bracket and cassette extractors, a chain cleaner, synthetic oil and a track pump capable of delivering the 90 pounds pressure that the tyres were running on, were also stowed in the camper van. I was told to run my tyres at over 100 pounds pressure but although that gave slightly less drag, I found the ride too uncomfortable. I dread to think what it must be like to ride on tyres at over 200 lbs. pressure, although I understand that they are usually confined to high speed track riding.

Psychology of journeys

Who do I ride with?

There is absolutely no doubt in my mind that support from significant others was a major factor in completing the ride. In sport, as in life, to be surrounded with negative messages is highly destructive, but to feel supported and encouraged is brilliant.

Perhaps it is a sign of maturity that some of us can choose not to spend time with people who are predominately negative. There are people I've met on life's journey about whom I would make such a choice, were I to encounter them now. In my work as a counsellor I may not have the same freedom of choice. Recognising and respecting people's choices in relation to me is equally important.

In my career with B.T. I had to spend years working with people who only saw the problems and not the possibilities, but I've left that life behind. However, when I first saw Lake Windermere through a gap in the hills on Day 12 of the ride, I was transported back to an outward bound type of course I attended for B.T. managers. On our first day we were taken across to the opposite bank of Windermere by road, put on to a small beach where we found some oil drums, ropes and planks and were told to get into two teams and construct rafts. The instructor pointed out our hotel across the water and said that dinner was waiting for us when we had paddled across. That sort of situation soon identifies the personality types! Very quickly we all learnt something about human behaviour, and not a little about how to tie knots!

I'll have a look at depression in another chapter but happiness, especially later in life, can be something to do with how we perceive the *Time Perspective*. This idea came from one of the 'ology' departments at Stanford University but despite that I quite like it! Let me explain: we all have a past, a present and a future, and we need all three, but if we become fixated on any one of these, then distortions can occur.

The *past negative* person is bitter about events in their past and continually ruminates on these. The *past positive* person tends to remain living in past glories with little awareness of other dimensions. The *present hedonist* is really only concerned about the here and now with little thought for the consequences, and the *present fatalist* is simply swept along by the tide and feels completely powerless. The remaining personality type is focused mainly on the *future,* being driven by an urgency to make lists, set goals and targets and exhibit a sense of urgency both within themselves and every one around them.

I saw all of these on the beach of Windermere. A conscious awareness of these traits and the ability, as it were, to smoothly change gear between them all can, I believe, help us to be more at peace with ourselves and be able to reflect our true values to those around us and to ourselves.

Why did I ride solo? There are lots of groups who cycle *end to end.* Was it because I didn't think I could keep up to their schedule or perversely and foolishly think that they might be too slow for me? No, none of these: I wanted to discover things about myself, not anyone else.

Mind Games

How did I psych myself up to ride a thousand miles in 20 days? Well, I didn't. I tried to think that the very most I had to cycle was 50 miles – and I knew I could do that: at least I've done 50 miles before.

Each day my only real goal was the first 10 miles. This type of goal setting is standard process when working with clients in counselling rooms – 'don't try boiling the ocean – try a spoonful at a time – go for what is attainable – be specific and congratulate yourself when it is accomplished'.

During the ride I would only focus on a close goal – a town, village, river or a time of day and aim for that, to be followed, perhaps, by a reward when achieved: a dried apricot, a drink or a rest. Even when I was very tired and wet, the positive thought of a large mug of hot tea and a shower and maybe even beating Carolyn at Scrabble that evening, minimised the 'why am I doing this ridiculous thing?' feeling.

I play golf, and one of my coping strategies for that activity is never to dwell on a bad shot, unlike some I know who throw their clubs about and utter expletives. Once a bad shot is played, it's in the past, I can't change it, but I can change the next shot and that is the key.

I was a climbing instructor a few years ago and the youngsters I was helping would almost always say, 'I can't get up there …you must be kidding,' or other such more colourful comment. However, once you told them to focus only on one move, the next handhold or ledge for their feet, and assured them they could do it, they became climbers and not sceptics.

Positive thinking is a great asset in sport as well as in life!

Old Habits

When scaling hills in Cornwall and Devon most of them suddenly appeared around a corner and little notice was given, so I had to be quick on the gear shifters or risk stalling. The problem here was that my *instinct* taught me to reach to the down tube for the gear levers which is where they were on the Holdsworth. I'd had 40 years of practice at that, and even though the gears were not index-linked I had no trouble in selecting the right one. On the *Trek* the gear shifters were incorporated into the brake levers, and more than once *my default setting*, of reaching down for a gear lever that wasn't there, made me feel a right wally!

In our daily living we all have ways of dealing with problems. Some may be entirely appropriate and effective, learnt over the years and come as second nature, our default setting that I mentioned earlier, but it does no harm to learn some new strategies. An example might be in the area of conflict. We may have learnt through our nurturing to walk away and feel badly treated, or perhaps the opposite, to rant and rave, stamp our feet and curse the offender. Perhaps we could learn how to confront the issue, without attacking the other person: stay calm, express our opinion, make our rights known, and seek resolution.

Another method that I used on my ride, in the daily mind game of climbing steep hills, was not to say, 'I can't ride up that.' Instead I would change the 'can't' to 'I choose not to' climb this hill. What this process does is to move our mindset from the negative towards the positive by giving us a choice. So the mind game goes on 'OK so I have a choice, actually I'll go a little bit further and see how I feel,' and so on.

I try this with some clients when I hear them say 'I can't possibly do that' by suggesting that they might like to change the expression to 'I choose not to do that.' This process can put them back in control of a hitherto insurmountable problem instead of the problem controlling them.

Another ploy, that always seems to create a little humour in the counselling room, is suggesting an alternative response to stressful situations. Let me explain. We might be confronted with a seemingly impossible amount of paper work on our desk or our boss has just put us down, or in my case on the ride I've just hit a pothole at 25 mph, nearly crashed and the front tyre has exploded.

Our natural response is to say or think, 'Oh no!', and allow despair, gloom or anger to engulf us. Whatever our response might be, our mind is sending messages to our body of alert or panic or despair, and all the chemicals start flowing to deal with the perceived threat. What we can do is change all those negative threatening messages by using an expression like, 'O that's interesting'; then the whole physiological response changes.

I've used this to great effect when slicing the odd golf ball out of bounds and I certainly used it on my ride when I got lost. In most cases we don't need adrenaline and cortisol pulsing through our veins to deal with the *majority* of our daily problems. When I hit the pothole my body would have automatically released stress hormones at an alarming rate, because quite rightly my brain had recognised a serious life-threatening situation. Some minutes after I had safely landed what I needed was clarity of thought, insight, perspective and imagination. I hope I said something like 'O that was interesting now what do I do,' however it might have been a more colourful phrase that I'm not recording here!

The humour within the counselling session arises when, for example, the client talks about some catastrophic work place encounter and imagines the response from his boss or colleagues when, for example, a multi million pound computer system crashes and he sits there and says, 'Oh that's interesting!' But it's amazing how many people do try this technique.

Humour within the counselling room is an entirely appropriate emotion. Although the walls of our counselling rooms are very well sound proofed, loud laughter can sometimes be heard through them. Laughter can be a highly effective therapeutic tool.

A Pat on The Back is No Bad Thing, but Difficult if You're on Your Own.

In the lakes and highlands hills didn't creep out on me round a bend: I could see them from miles away or else I had been warned about them in the guide book or seen a sign on the road side warning of *road closure due to thick snow during adverse weather* – this latter always a subtle way of indicating that a climb was round the corner! How did I manage the hills? I found that to focus just on the next mile or a landmark was my way of climbing them – not to look at the peak. Sometimes I might just sneak a look and my heart would sink. But it was always a rewarding experience to reach the top and to say out loud, 'Well done, you made it!'

Isn't it great when people say to us well done. How often do we say to those we love, 'You've done a great job there, thank you'?

In some of the couples counselling I've been involved with, it's amazing how often the bread-winner is taken for granted for bringing home the money every month, and how much the bread-winner takes for granted the work of the home-maker or the partner who looks after the children. It's really great to see the couple acknowledge each other for this most fundamental but important part of their journey together.

What is Counselling? Does it Help?

John Barnes, the Vicar of Longfield's husband, who is a real cyclist and rang me every day of my journey, was a great support. I knew when I talked about the pain and the fatigue, that he had been there, many times, and his help made a difference. He said I would get stronger not weaker as the journey progressed, and that I would lose weight: he was right on both counts.

However counselling is *not* about finding someone who has experienced all of life's traumas or even some of them. It is fundamentally about a relationship with another human being who, above all other things, listens in a very special way.

Jonathan Sacks, the Chief Rabbi, tells the story of his fellow Jew, Victor Frankl, to whom I referred earlier. A woman phoned him in the middle of the night and calmly told him that she was about to commit suicide. Frankl kept her on the telephone and talked her through her depression, giving her reason after reason to carry on living. Eventually she promised him she would not take her life, and she kept her word. When they met later, Frankl asked her which of his reasons she had found convincing. 'None', she replied. What then persuaded her to go on living? Her answer was simple. Frankl had been willing to listen to her in the middle of the night. A world in which someone was prepared to listen to another's distress seemed to her one in which it was worthwhile to live.

What an underrated art listening is. Sometimes it is the greatest gift we can give to a troubled soul. It is an act of focused attention. It means being genuinely open to another person, prepared to enter their world, their perspective, and their pain. It does not mean that we have a solution to their problem. There are some problems that cannot be solved. They can only be lived through, so that time itself heals the rupture or loss. When we listen, we share the burden so that its weight can be borne.

There are times when friendship calls simply for a human presence, a listening ear and an understanding heart, so that soul can unburden itself to soul.

Carl Rogers, the father of humanistic counselling, described those special qualities needed for the therapeutic alliance to be effective. He said there needed to be unconditional positive regard, congruence and empathy on the part of the therapist. Many post-Rogers writers would agree but add that essential as those qualities are, they are insufficient on their own for therapy to be effective. Within the counselling profession there are many different theoretical models whose exponents might claim to be the best. At one end there are the analytical theories of Freud and Yung. This therapy is likely to be prolonged, and deep-searching. A long way from Freud is De-Shazer who designed Solution Focused Brief Therapy. This process is time limited, probably four to six sessions, and the counsellor's job is to keep the client looking at possibilities and not problems: a better future, not a troubled past: the client's strengths and not his weaknesses. In between these two extremes are many other systems; most have considerable merit and in the hands of a skilled helper most clients will benefit.

'It's a funny thing,' said Rabbit ... 'how everything looks the same in a mist. Have you noticed it Pooh?' Most people seeking help see life as if in a mist. Extending the meteorological analogy a little more, try thinking of the counselling systems not as a shopping basket – I don't like shopping anyway – but as colours of the same rainbow. I'm not really sure where I fit in on the rainbow colour chart but hope that some of my clients might echo the words of the woman in the story told by Jonathan Sacks.

Along with many other males of the species, I really detest shopping; for me it is a real chore, coming a close third behind paying income tax and having teeth pulled. Imagine the pain I go through when working in the counselling room with clients who presented with agoraphobia or panic attacks and have discovered coping strategies for going out. They might want to spend the *whole* counselling hour telling me how they went from shop to shop to supermarket to garden centre and even the D.I.Y. superstore.

I can exhibit genuine empathy as they tell their story!

People often ask whether counsellors give advice. The answer should be no. It might be appropriate sometimes to give information; however the problem with giving advice is, if it is wrong we will have harmed the client and if it is right, every time the client needs to make a decision they will be knocking on our door. The best scenario is to create a climate in which the client becomes empowered to make his own decisions and to own them. The counsellor's job then would be to commiserate or celebrate the outcome with his client.

Counselling is certainly about exploring *choices*, but it might also be about *change* as well. An expression I sometimes use to help a client see why changing a pattern of behaviour might be helpful is this: *If you always do what you've always done, you'll always get what you always got.* This might be stating the obvious, but so often people in therapy are not seeing issues too clearly and might feel that they are going round in circles and want to break out. It's a bit like learning *not* to apply the front brake of a bike too hard going round a bend on a wet road. You'll almost always fall off!

The words used by one client in describing her therapist were these:

'He gave me freedom to cry
The oomph to fly
And helped me find ten reasons not to die.'

Going Down... It Can Become Addictive

Climbing the hill was, of course, only part of the story; going down presents different but equally demanding challenges. During a descent on the Tour de France one cyclist developed such heat on his wheels from the road surface and his brakes that the adhesive holding the tyre to the rim melted, the tyre came off and the rider suffered multiple fractures after crashing on to the road.

My own downhill problems manifested themselves whilst still in Cornwall. My hands became blistered because of repeatedly having to apply the brakes on the very severe hills, and this despite wearing padded cycling gloves.

I learnt something new about downhill riding whilst watching the Tour de France on television. At the summit of major descents bystanders would offer the cyclists newspapers. The riders would push them inside the front of their jerseys, and then on arriving at the bottom of the hill, discard them. This, of course, provided them with insulation against the cold. I experienced the dramatic effects of sudden cold during several descents, especially in Scotland when it was wet. It was so serious on one occasion that, although I found a garage selling hot drinks, I was shaking so much I couldn't operate the dispenser. Fortunately, a kindly garage assistant rescued me.

The downhill spiral for many people involves the issue of addiction. This is one of the toughest areas to confront in the area of psychological distress. That is why the great organisation Alcoholics Anonymous talks of *recovering alcoholics* and not of *cured alcoholics*. They recognise the very thin thread that holds a person with addictive tendencies from falling back into the grip of their addiction. The director of a local private clinic suggests that some people are predisposed towards addictive behaviour. He said that the best his clinic could offer these people would be to help them move from an addiction that would lead to an early grave, towards other addictive behaviours that could be lived with. I'll have a closer look at addiction in another chapter.

I remember one man whose addiction to alcohol was threatening both his marriage and his job. He managed to divert his addiction from the bottle to trainers. He had a dormant sporting gene and really did become hooked on running to a point at which it was quite obsessive, but the last time I heard he was still married and had kept his job.

A Story in Five Short Chapters

For some clients with addictive tendencies this has helped.

Chapter 1

I walk down the street.
There is a deep hole in the sidewalk.
I fall in.
I am lost ...I am helpless.
It isn't my fault.
It takes forever to find a way out.

Chapter 2

I walk down the same street.
There is a deep hole in the sidewalk.

I pretend I don't see it.
I fall in again.
I can't believe I am in the same place.
But it isn't my fault.
It takes a long time to get out.

Chapter 3
I walk down the same street.
There is a deep hole in the sidewalk.
I see it is there.
I still fall in … it's a habit.
My eyes are open.
I know where I am.
It is my fault.
I get out immediately.

Chapter 4
I walk down the same street.
There is a deep hole in the sidewalk.
I walk around it.

Chapter 5
I walk down another street.

Portia Nelson

Pornography and Paedophilia

One of the emergent addictions that I have listened to is in the area of Internet pornography. Many men have talked about the hold this has on them; I suspect that what I have heard is just the tip of a very big iceberg. However, like most addictions, these cause break-up in relationships, feelings of intense loneliness and despair as well as loss of job. I've worked with several men whose personal computer (P.C.) at work had been found to contain images downloaded from pornographic sites. Although they thought the images had been deleted, when their employers made security checks on their P.C., as they frequently do within industry, they had some explaining to do.

I have spent 35 years working in industry and most of that was male dominated. The girly magazines were very much part of the culture, and exposure to them on a regular basis was commonplace. Whilst not condoning them or the associated exploitation of women, I do not believe that they corrupted a generation. Some men were undoubtedly affected by them and in a way the same problem exists today. The sale of the magazines has declined in inverse proportion to the increase in use of the internet. It is a problem, and some men, and to a lesser extent women, with addictive tendencies will become hooked on internet pornography rather than pornographic magazines. Will this present trend corrupt a generation?

An article in *Idea,* the resource magazine for members of the evangelical alliance, disclosed that in a recent survey in America 40% of pastors had visited a pornographic website. CARE, the Christian organisation, is getting so many calls from British Christians that it recently took the step of publishing online resources for fighting pornography addiction. Although I am not aware of any statistics from Britain, in America half of all churchgoers admit to personal struggles with pornography.

Elaine Storkey, in her book *The Search for Intimacy* says, 'The saddest thing is that pornography can never be a substitute for relating to another human being. It can only widen the loneliness.' Most of the men I have worked with in the counselling room would relate to that.

Our society has rightly decided that the abuse of children by paedophiles is a very serious offence, but when I am sitting in the counselling room with a person convicted of such awful deeds I usually just see a person with an addiction from which there seems no escape. Almost always there is a history of abuse in the childhood of such people. I am definitely not trying to excuse them, or produce evidence to justify what these people do, but the perpetrators of these crimes are *addicted* in a similar way to drug addicts or alcoholics.

As a father and a grandfather, I would not be too sure how I would respond if one of these people ever abused a member of my family.

Three of the Gospels record the words of Jesus to the effect that it would be better to have a great millstone fastened round one's neck and be drowned in the depth of the sea than to harm a child. I find the actions of paedophiles unforgivable but have to suspend those feelings in the work I do, and trust in my God and the legal system to dispense justice. I know how dirty I feel after just *hearing* the story from an abuser; I cannot begin to imagine what the victims must feel like.

Unfortunately we do not have showers at the counselling centre and just scrubbing my hands and face after such sessions still leaves me feeling contaminated.

If counsellors, in the course of their work, ever suspect that children may be at risk then they have a legal responsibility to report their suspicions. The client would be told this at the outset of counselling.

These problems really are fast downhill journeys and for many people, the brakes seem to be totally ineffective, and the wheels really do fall off with catastrophic consequences.

Although I have linked pornography and paedophilia in the same heading, my experience suggests that while most paedophiles, certainly in recent times, may have kick-started their evil deeds via the internet, I am *not* suggesting that all the people who access pornography are paedophiles. Most of the people I've worked with in this area are as repulsed by that material as I would be.

What can be done then, for people with this problem of addiction? One of the key hurdles is understanding that most of those afflicted are in denial of the problem. 'Oh yes, I do drink a bit but it's not a problem, I could give up tomorrow if I wanted to,' they say. Heavy smokers know that cigarettes kill but choose to push the knowledge to the back of their minds.

If you try and force the person to see the truth, then failure is almost guaranteed. Remember that denial is a self-defence mechanism so to challenge somebody in denial is very likely going to make them more defensive.

The beginning of hope occurs when the person struggling with the problem is able to admit that they have a problem and they are able to see for themselves the reality of their plight. Sometimes this will mean the person getting into a very perilous condition and then, although rescuing them might seem the natural act of a compassionate carer, it will come to nought unless the person himself has the inward desire to change.

Spirituality of Journeys

The Spirit Was Willing. But ...

It would be quite appropriate to say of me and my journey that the spirit was willing for only parts of the journey and the flesh was weak for most of it!

I have always liked Psalm 8 because of the way it describes us as being 'a little lower than the angels'. I sort of feel comfortable there! I know that David, the writer of the Psalm, was certainly a bit lower than most of the angels I know – quite significantly so at times – but in the New Testament he is described as being 'a man after God's own heart'. Considering some of David's exploits I take great heart from that. David also talks in that Psalm about his world. He didn't, I realise, have the North Sea or the Highlands of Scotland in mind, but his words capture the feelings of wonder just the same.

It was a very moving experience, when we visited the Holy Land on another journey, to be shown what commentators believe to be the valley that David describes in Psalm 23:

'Though I walk in the valley of the shadow of death ... '. Apparently there are places in the valley that the sun never reaches. So David was very aware of what he was saying in describing what he must have felt like in his low times.

So, back to the journey – the spiritual and the *end to end* – yes, there were lots of doubts and lots of pain, in various places.

My spiritual struggle has always been, and still is, with the Christians and churches who seem to emit the greatest light. So often in my own spiritual journey the people I have seen from a distance as holy and good, and I'm not just referring to people six foot above contradiction standing in the pulpit, are far from that close up. Quite large chunks of their lives seem to have been, or still are, lived out in the dark shadows of the valleys.

In my counselling work I soon discovered that quite often those people and those churches who appeared to create the brightest light so often also cast the darkest shadow. Perhaps it is 'man thing' but although I have a wide circle of really good male friends I've never really had a close brother type of relationship. Perhaps it is for that reason my spiritual journey has become quite a solitary one – like my ride.

Don't Look Back, Just Focus on One Day.

I remember Colin, my friend who runs Marathons, asking me, a couple of weeks before we set out, if I had woken up yet and thought, 'why am I doing this?' I suppose I did on the morning we left for St Agnes Bay in Cornwall, which was to be our overnight stop before Land's End. Not only was I thinking, 'Why am I doing this?', but also, 'Why have I got Carolyn involved in this foolhardy exploit? She has plenty of challenges without this.' I guess a little bit of having put your hand to the plough, don't turn back, kicked in.

Every morning of the ride I would be up early and sit outside the camper van, while Carolyn gently dozed within, having had a cup of something made by me first. I would just meditate: read about the journey ahead for that day in the excellent ride handbook, sometimes read a Psalm, or just be.

I had a feeling that the author of the ride book might be a Christian. He always focused on any spiritual dimension of places on the route – for example using the words of Matthew 26, which describes the institution of the Lord's supper, and suggesting a link with the legend of Joseph of Arimathea bringing the cup to Glastonbury. All the major cathedrals and shrines were mentioned with great attention to detail.

I really did try and apply the idea of not worrying about the morrow, as we are told in the Gospels and yes, the 'birds of the air and the lilies of the fields' really did look great, just as it says in Matthew's gospel. I really admire people who apply that theology to their daily living, but I find the concept hard to embrace.

Carolyn's Day

Plan A for our adventure was that Carolyn would use the time while I was cycling to make inroads into her research project for her theology diploma. She was writing a paper on *The Spiritual Care of the Dying*. We both thought this would be a highly appropriate subject considering our reservations about my own ability to complete the ride. However that part of the plan was not entirely successful. There was not too much time left in the day after seeing me off to work on my bike in the morning and then having to pack up the camper van, get the shopping, navigate and find the new camp site, 50 miles or more away. She then had to set up the van again, before a hot sweaty and tired cyclist arrived. Some progress was made but not as much as Carolyn had hoped.

Each evening Carolyn had to try and find a campsite in one of the site handbooks, that was not too far from my cycle route the next day, and also about 50 miles north. We then had to work out how I could find the site. Only once did she meet me en route and that was in Dumfries. The site she had chosen was about 10 miles off my route and I would already have cycled about 70 miles that day. We had several camp site books with us and because we were travelling outside school holidays did not need to book ahead. She did a great job and really got a feel for what was right for us.

For me it was simply a case of where she leads I will follow and what she feeds I will swallow.

Theological Potholes

I'm not exposed to mortal danger much these days but over 42 mph on one occasion on the bike did make me reflect a little on what it would be like to wake up dead. Sure there had to be an end to my journey – whether the planned one at John O'Groats or some other place en route. And sure enough life's mortal journey will also end one day – time and place also unknown.

My own faith in Jesus convinces me that this will not be the end of that journey. I hope that some of the people I've met along my life's journey, who also share the Christian faith, will not be on my wheel, to use a cycling expression! It was painful enough spending time with them on earth where I could walk away; the thought of spending eternity with them is not high on my wish list. I sense some deep theological issues about forgiveness emerging here! There are, however, many, many other people with whom I very much hope to share that part of my journey.

The notion of predestination is an issue I've wrestled with many times. Does our God predestine that such a journey, any journey, will end in success? Some I know would say, 'Of course!' And my journey did end in success, but I do not put that down to predestination. My faith is real to me but that doesn't alter the fact that the choices and responsibilities on my journey were mine and mine alone – like not applying my brakes as the speed indicator of my bike hit 40 mph!

I'm watching the Tour de France whilst writing this and seeing the horrific injuries that those young cyclists incur when crashing at 50 mph plus, does tend to focus my mind on the dangers of cycling. I know that the physiology of thrill produces highs for the adrenaline junkies, and that is what keeps them doing what they do. But I'm not into that and I don't think I ever was.

In relating that to the spiritual journey, I'm very aware that mountain top experiences cannot be sustained indefinitely, and the Psalms remind me very much of the valleys which is where most of us, I suspect, spend a fair bit of our time.

The lowest point of my ride came after climbing the Kirkstone Pass in Cumbria,the highest pass in England. I arrived at the campsite on the banks of Ullswater completely exhausted to find that midges had attacked Carolyn as she arrived at the site. She was in a poor way, so I went back to Pooley Bridge, the village at the end of the lake, and found out that a boat was doing a cruise on the lake. We had a really pleasant evening away from the midges ... but we were only half way to John O' Groats!

When we woke up the following morning the inside of the van was coated with the wee beasties and we had to scrape them off the windows!

I've spent many counselling sessions with people from what is known as the happy clappy end of the Christian spectrum. They might want to explore why they sometimes feel low. They believe that because they are the Salt of the Earth following the Light of the World then they shouldn't feel low or depressed. Unfortunately this message is sometimes reinforced from the pulpits but joy and peace may seem like distant mirages to the client I'm working with. The irony of this is that the next client might be a church leader saying that the message he is delivering to his flock is a travesty because his life is all screwed up.

Oh for more honesty, less fantasy, more realism and less make-believe! The Jesus I know does not walk about with a smile permanently etched on his face. I certainly didn't have one etched on mine during my ride.

So Ullswater was a low point, but if I had had to quit anywhere this would have been a pretty place in which to do it, however the midges did rather take the shine off our time there.

I am very aware that the aforementioned theological potholes are fertile ground for my academic Christian friends to think that not only have I fallen off my bike again but probably off my perch as well. They might want to pick me up, dust me off, put me back on my bike, give me a gentle push and send me off in the *right* direction. Thanks anyway but I'll manage on my own, this time, but I might fall off again, so stay in touch!

Broken Spokes and Buckled Wheels???

I did a sponsored bike ride for the Ellenor Foundation on the Brands Hatch Grand Prix track several years ago. I had not realised from watching the car and motorcycle races on television just how hilly the circuit was. I had not ridden my bike a great deal prior to the event; I certainly wasn't very fit and after a couple of laps I discovered that my old bike wasn't really up for it either. Whilst descending one of the hills, with a sharp bend half way down, my rear wheel made a cracking noise and several spokes snapped and the wheel buckled. Fortunately I was able to complete the ride by releasing the rear brake sufficiently to allow the buckled rim to pass.

Of all the issues that have polarised Christian thinking over the years and especially in recent times, apart, that is from the ordination of women, the virgin birth and the resurrection, human sexuality must be very near the top of the list.

Vast swathes of the evangelicals consider anybody with sexual feelings outside of what is thought as straight, to be fallen and broken spirits, who should repent of their sin and be forgiven for their fallen state.

The Anglicans seem to be much like my bike with the buckled wheel. They continue to function despite the problems, by keeping their heads down, making a few adjustments and hoping no one notices. Even if they do spot a problem they'll almost certainly ignore it and hope it goes away.

As far as the Catholics are concerned they seem, in general, to be in denial that anything is remotely wrong at all.

Significant numbers of all the above still refuse to allow women, per se, to hold any positions of authority within their Church. I'm not talking global here, this is happening in my own village. Perhaps, however, Meopham is unusual; not all the churches will even walk together as a faith witness on Good Friday. I can eat soup and a roll in one Church but not receive communion. I despair!

Having now alienated most of my Christian readers I hope my friends of other faiths and no faith will read on!

One of the interesting aspects of working with people who seek psychological help is the difference between *presenting issues* and *emergent issues.*

More often than not what a client will talk about in the initial session will only be, at best, part of the problem, and more than likely be covering much deeper concerns. Only when the relationship with the therapist has matured, and the client feels safe will other issues emerge ... usually in the last five minutes of the session ... doctors call this *the hand on the door syndrome*. They describe how a patient who perhaps presented with a painful big toe and was just leaving the consulting room will say something like *'Oh and by the way I've been having some chest pain, extending down my arms accompanied by severe vomiting and profuse sweating'!*

Quite often those deeper feelings will be about sexuality. I have worked with several women who presented with problems within their marriage, and what has emerged has been a relationship outside the marriage which has given them joy, peace and love. Sometimes this relationship has been with another woman.

I have worked with many men who have tried and tried to fight their instincts and find meaningful relationships with women but find no solace there, and are continually drawn like magnets towards other men. I have shared time with men who find immense relief in dressing in women's clothes. Others who believed that they were women trapped in male bodies, and much rarer, in my experience, women who thought they should have been men. I have not been able, during my time in this work, ever to see these people as broken or bent or in need of repair.

The homosexuals I know simply do not see their sexuality as their defining characteristic. They may be priests, teachers, musicians, doctors, bank clerks or engineers. They are not *defined* by their sexuality any more than the majority of us are, who find our sexual friendships in the opposite gender.

Extending the debate into the area of gay rights and whether same sex marriage and the rights of such couples to be parents should be recognised, is another issue. I do know through my own experiences of working with the abused, that many heterosexual couples are not fit to parent children.

I firmly believe that children develop best within a loving family comprising a mother and father. Alongside that I have to recognise that well over 40% of all marriages now end in divorce. A child psychiatrist friend from America says that of all the children he has worked with, presenting with A.D.D. (attention deficit disorder) or similar complaints, over 99% will have endured, or are enduring, some sort of emotional trauma in their family life. So what we do with the complex issue of human sexuality in our spiritual journey I'm not really sure. I know I had to buy a new rear wheel for my bike after Brands Hatch. If only life was that simple!

Off The Road For a While

I mentioned earlier about the journey being painful and there were times when the ride really hurt but that pain is transient. On our life journey the painful times are not so easily erased.

I suppose the death of our first child was one of the first major losses.

The death of my grandparents was obviously significant; I knew all four of them right through my formative years: I enjoyed them all and can see now how they helped form the person I am today. Grandparents reading this ... you are very important, do not underestimate your influence.

My Dad died after some difficult years for us all, when the quality of his life had really diminished. He did show amazing resilience however having had his larynx removed many years before. In reality he died of the diseases of old age although the medics are reluctant to put that on the death certificate, I'll look more at this issue later on.

Certainly when our baby Sarah died I really had no idea what was happening, but sad to reflect, nobody else seemed to know what to do either. Even the caring professionals around at the time seemed to distance themselves from our grief. I seem to recall that the GP who attended Carolyn at the time later committed suicide ... not connected with our events directly so far as I am aware.

That part of the journey did have a happy ending when Emma, Judith and Kingsley, our children, arrived in early 70s. We had a great time with them and our peer group in Gravesend and later at Darenth Grange, the residential care home Carolyn helped to run.

I only hope that I have been of more help to others in difficult situations. I know that Carolyn has.

Brief Camp Site Stop Over

It was on our very first site at St.Agnes Bay in Cornwall that Carolyn was used to help someone else on their journey. The lady who owned the farm told Carolyn how her husband had suffered a tragic death related to an industrial accident on the farm. It sounded horrible. He had ingested some diesel fuel and died a painful death. Carolyn only went to the shop to buy a pint of milk, but happened to be in the right place at the right time.

The same thing happened in Cumbria, when Carolyn met another lady, whose husband had recently died and needed to tell her story.

I know that not everyone can be a good listener, but within Christian tradition there is a great heritage of people able to offer those skills ...what sort of listener are you? ... do you want to learn more?

A Small B Road Diversion Off The Spiritual A Road

The beginning of the journey of my working life seemed to be on rails ... almost automatic – along with many others from Erith Technical School, we had interviews at Vickers at Crayford, Halls at Dartford and Fraser and Chalmers at Erith. I was offered apprenticeships at them all. However Frasers was accepted because it offered a sandwich course involving studying for a National Diploma in Mechanical Engineering.

I can remember having to get up very early to clock on at 7.30 a.m. and Mum getting my breakfast before I cycled off. The journey was only slightly longer than the journey to school.

I really did not like the environment in the machine shops. It was dirty, noisy and hot and really quite frightening – enormous machines, overhead hoists clattering along gantries 30 feet or so above ground and massive chains and hooks. I remember finding this environment very hostile and did not enjoy it. I think this career move was from my Dad's side of the family but it was from my Mum's side that the next move was born.

My Grandad had recently retired from the Post Office. He was an engineer in the telephony division of that organisation. Although I can't remember all the details, I had an interview at London Bridge to become an apprentice in Post Office Telecommunications.

My first day was at Erith Telephone Exchange. I remember feeling OK about that. The strange irony is that I was the manager there when the mechanical automatic equipment was eventually switched off in 1991. It still smelt the same all those years later – yes, Telephone Exchanges have a very distinctive smell, along with most other engineering plants.

Sometimes when working with clients we use the five senses of sight, sound, touch, taste and smell to recapture memories and feelings not only of trauma but of happy times as well.

One of the joys of cycling is to be able to use the senses of smell, sound and taste usually not available from within a car. My ride along the banks of the Cromarty Firth with the Moray Firth beyond, highlighted this with the smell of the whisky distilleries, the taste of salt on my lips and ferocity of the westerly gales blowing in my face … it was wonderful

End of Diversion
Back on The Spiritual Road

I am reminded of the words used by Tim Moore in his excellent little book, *French Revolutions* – about the Tour de France, lent to me by Dr Andrew from the Ellenor Foundation. He describes what it was like for him, a humble journalist, after climbing the Col de Saraille in the Pyrenees at over 900 metres altitude. He said 'my heart felt like bursting and that it was a religious experience: I am healed; I can see; in conquering the savage beauty around me I have, in fact, become its creator. The climb had not been a Calvary but a road to Damascus, one that had converted me to a self-believer. For the first time in over twenty years I raised both my hands from a set of handlebars and punched the blue sky.'

For me, the Kirkstone Pass in the Lake District was that. I had nothing to prove to the world, but something to prove to myself – and yes, I did punch the air, but I only used one fist! The highest pass in England and I'd done it!

What, however of the one hill I did not climb? The one out of Loch Ness, no … not the loch … but the valley, I failed. Did I? Well, I certainly discovered my limitations. I ran out of gears … all 27 of them, devoid of energy, breath, and stamina. I gave it everything I had on that day, in that place, at that time. There just wasn't anything left – not a single unburned calorie, the tank was empty.

I know John Barnes would have made it whilst still chatting about the weather – probably without so much as a drop of sweat, or is it perspiration in Longfield? I'd reached my limit.

At the time it seemed a bit sad that one climb on my journey had been too great, but on reflection that seems OK. Perhaps it's one of many human failings that we too often measure our achievements by other people's standards and not be comfortable with who we are as children of God made in his image.

Parenting and Suffering, Not Always Connected!

An enduring problem for many people who seek psychological help is the sense of failure, gift wrapped and handed on to them by their parents. I remember one couple who said it started with a speech at the wedding reception with some cruel words from her father; continued while on honeymoon when the parents went to their house, unwrapped all the presents and put everything away ... just so the house would be nice and tidy when they got back. Things got even worse when the couple had children, with a controlling mother-in-law criticising every move. When the young lady did ask her mother for help she was told that most marriages were a disaster and she would just have to put up with it.

Part of being a parent is the ability to let go and allow the child to become the adult, and to celebrate if the child *isn't* a clone of the parent but has developed a way of being that is unique to themselves.

Much has been written about suffering especially within the context of a loving God. I've heard so many sermons justifying God's wrath on sinful people that I am now almost immune to that concept. I simply do not believe illness and suffering are God's free gifts for not walking the narrow way. I am so glad that Jesus did not *always* link sin and illness although he did on some occasions!

My own journey has brought me to an understanding based loosely around the existentialist notion that to live is to suffer and to survive is to find meaning in the suffering. As Nietzsche said 'he who has a *why* to live can bear with almost any *how*'.

I know that the German philosopher who said that was not a Christian sympathiser, but I prefer his understanding about suffering to a great deal of what is offered by some Christian commentators. Christopher Reeve, the American actor who played Superman, was quoted as saying 'suffering is inevitable, misery is a choice'. He said this after being paralysed for life after a riding accident.

If there is any purpose in life at all then there must be a purpose in suffering and dying. The key, I believe, is that we must each make our personal response to these concepts.

Lance Armstrong, a survivor of cancer, writing in his book *Every Second Counts,* gives his perspective on suffering. He talks about his suffering in winning the Tour de France for the second time, how his neck became thin and his ribs and shoulder blades jutted out of his shirt because of massive weight loss. He believed that because he suffered more, his win and survival were all the more gratifying. He felt suffering was essential to a good life. He explains how for him he grew as a human being through his suffering and not just physically but inside himself as well. He felt the reward for his pain was self-knowledge; if he had quit he felt the pain would have lasted forever and that knowledge kept him going both through his illness and in his riding. I am pleased that Armstrong did not say that if he had *lost,* the pain would have lasted forever. There is sort of spiritual, Olympic ideal about not quitting, but that does not always mean we will be winners either in sport or in life.

I believe that a great deal of our suffering is spread across clearly defined areas of our lives. These areas may be defined as our *emotions*, our *education and employment*, our *physical well-being*, our *environment ... home and society* and *our spirituality*. It can be helpful to identify which of these it might be suitable to work on. Most clients already know what it is about their way of being that is not really functioning. Allowing people time to explore can be the start of the healing process.

For people who work with the dying one of the commonest stories they hear is about unresolved guilt, anger and resentment. So often it is only on the deathbed that these issues are confronted. For these people healing can bring some meaning to the end of their lives. For those of us not on our deathbed then healing can bring a life that has meaning before its end and a *well done good and faithful servant* when our time comes.

Physiology of Journeys

Linking Our Minds and Bodies

Pedalling like mad and going nowhere ... a bit like an exercise bike in the gym is what it felt like for me some years ago.

There were serious issues within my time as a manager with B.T. and these culminated in an illness that I think captures the well known link between our minds and our bodies – ***the psychosomatic dimension.***

I had been exposed to some psychological pressure just before going into management in the late 1970s. The engineering union, which I had joined at the start of my career, was calling us out on strike. I refused to withdraw my labour but offered to donate my earnings to charity. This offer was rejected at a kangaroo court held while I was on holiday, and I was expelled from the union. I was *marked out* for quite a time after that, and only really escaped the cold shoulder treatment when I left the engineering ranks after promotion into management.

It was in the mid 1980s that several factors combined to create feelings of hopelessness for me. I was embroiled in conflict at work with yet another new line management structure; the performance of the telephone exchanges that I ran became linked to my pay and more strikes were looming.

I discovered, almost by accident, that my new in line senior managers, who were now based in another area, were all Freemasons and I had been given a poor appraisement, which of course affected my salary and ultimately my pension. I had made steady, if unspectacular, progress as a manager, had a staff of about forty, and was well respected by my peers.

The performances of my telephone exchanges were excellent. I had a very good team, some of whom are still friends today. To be confronted with an appraisement that was so far removed from the truth, was shattering. However, to go to appeal and find it dismissed out of hand, caused me to do a little digging and ask questions. It was then I discovered the Masonic link through the management hierarchy. I was warned not to make waves, but my competitive persona kicked in and I took them on and won but it was a messy encounter and I think I was the only casualty. I'm sorry if any Masons read this but my discoveries highlighted corruption and conspiracy in high places and I make no apologies for choosing those words. *I know Free Masonry does a lot of good community work, but along with other Christian colleagues over the years I have really struggled with this issue and despite having friends who are Masons, I have never really come to terms with just where their loyalty is rooted.*

At the same time as this, my parents were coping with serious illness; we were moving house; we had three teenage children and the church I was attending gave me more grief than peace. I remember buying a sticker for my car during this time; it was a Christian one and had a picture of a woolly sheep and the words 'The Lord is my Shepherd'. I felt a bit like the lost sheep, certainly not part of a flock, but fortunately never too far from the shepherd.

Did you know that bike riders who cycle in a group either socially or in a race do so mainly because, like birds when flying in formation, they use 15% less energy than cycling solo? Aren't birds clever!

This lost sheep developed severe abdominal pains – had tubes put up and down but nothing showed up so the medics decided it must be a grumbling appendix. I went into Benenden Hospital, while the Tour de France was on Channel 4 television, and had the appendix removed. I remember the surgeon coming round afterwards and saying that there was nothing wrong with it, but he took it out just the same!

I know they say you can't remember pain, but I was in considerable discomfort on the journey home from hospital – and, no, it wasn't Carolyn's driving. I had developed an infection in the wound – a sort of early MRSA bug and was off work for several more weeks. I can still remember my deputy visiting me at home, not to enquire about my health of course, but to resolve some work problems! I know now that my body was reacting to the stress in my life but no one at the time connected up all the bits.

Stress Issues – Getting The Right Pressure in The System.

From what I hear in the counselling room from countless burnt out south-east men and women, not a lot has changed on the stress front in the last 20 years, apart from the sales of antidepressants or other forms of chemical dependency, some prescribed, many others not!

The subject of stress is still hitting the headlines; more days were lost at work in 2002 due to stress than any other single condition, even back pain. Some stress is a necessary part of motivational conditioning. Without it we do not perform to our potential.

So what is stress? It is the body's natural reaction to threat i.e. the flight or fight response. We are programmed biologically, when confronted with danger, either to confront it or escape from it. Our bodies produce adrenaline and cortisol amongst other chemicals; our minds go on alert, our blood clotting ability increases, in case we are injured, and blood supply increases to our muscles to enable us to run or fight.

A very simplistic description might be to think of stress in terms of a bicycle tyre and inner tube. If you have ever ridden a bike with really soft tyres then it is very hard work; you don't get too far, generate a lot of heat and you soon feel pretty worn out. This is what is known sometimes as passive stress, because we are under-stimulated. However when the correct amount of pressure is applied to the inner tube then the tyre sits snugly on the rim, and you sail along really well. The ride is pleasant. Sure there are some uphill bits and also some easy freewheel times but we usually arrive at our destination in reasonable shape. Over-inflate the tyre and there is even bigger trouble ahead; risk of, at worst exploding, but always a very bumpy ride and the wear across the tyre is uneven and so its useable mileage is considerably reduced.

During my time as a redeployment counsellor with B.T., I dealt with many cases of passive stress. Most of the staff I was working with had been the backbone of the electro-mechanical-electronic switching systems for over thirty years. They were clever, highly motivated and well trained engineers who suddenly found themselves without a job because of the advent of digital switching which required much lower staffing levels. The company, to its credit, had committed itself to a no compulsory redundancy policy. I remember one group of these highly trained, motivated, clever individuals being given the job of painting floors beneath the wiring frames in telephone exchanges. The concept was a good one: if the floors were painted white then there would be better reflection from the artificial overhead lighting thus creating a brighter working environment for the staff working on the frames. So far so good.

The problem was, they painted too quickly, much quicker than planned and there was a significant risk of them running out of work. One of their managers decided to issue them with smaller brushes. 'That should slow them down a bit,' I heard him say. This was just one of many examples of how to de-motivate people.

The physiological responses described earlier all occur when we are under stress. However the threats creating the stress are not those that usually require the body to react in the way it is programmed to do. So the chemicals, the stress hormones cortisol and adrenaline within our blood stream, are not dissipated; our bodies remain on alert and if this cycle is continued day after day then we start on the road to *distress*.

What Are The Tell Tale Signs of Stress?

There are several ways to identify whether this characteristic of *stress becoming distress is* happening. We may not be sleeping too well because, if our bodies perceive a physical threat, then sleep is not a good survival mechanism! We may be reacting to interpersonal or relationship problems in an uncharacteristically hostile way. Once again, our bodies are not historically well equipped in the use of negotiating skills when we are about to be attacked by a man-eating tiger! We might be drinking more alcohol, smoking either tobacco or one of the hallucinogenic compounds; these are good ways of coping, but the side effects are problematic tending towards fatal. Comfort-eating is another escape chute for some; lack of concentration, forgetfulness, digestive problems, inability to relax, obsessional behaviour, staying late at work and/or bringing work home on a regular basis, are all further clues of a stressful life.

It could be that we don't take holidays. I worked with managers who used to brag about how much leave they had left over at the end of the year – a coded way of saying that they were so important to the company that they could not possibly be away from their desks. Someone said in a book about family life, ' Who on his tombstone would want the words engraved, "I wish I had spent more time at the office!" ' Any, or all of the above, may be clues to a life style that is too stressed.

Riding a Tandem – a Bicycle Made For Two

There are several well-tried and tested methods of dealing with the problems of stress but this little book is not the place for all of those. Three of the most common coping strategies involve relaxation or meditation techniques, laughter therapy, which produces endorphins, the body's very own happy drug, and exercise. Plenty of evidence exists to support all three of these coping mechanisms but to highlight just one will suffice for now.

A study from Harvard looked at individuals who had lived for over 100 years, just one in 10,000 of us. A lively sense of humour was a notable skill among these Human Volvos. The study found that these people had a keen wit, a sense of humour, and a creative and flexible approach to life's slings and arrows. The accumulated evidence showed clearly that laughter isn't just a luxury; it's a fundamental building block to all round health and happiness. So when you're devising ways to bring more laughter into your life, do remember that we're 30 times more likely to laugh when we're in company than on our own – just another example of how Mother Nature is urging us to team up and enjoy life. A fertile bond can be a great source of joy and create positive emotions. It can enable us to flourish and grow beyond ourselves. If it is not possible for that bond to be with another person then perhaps a place or a skill or a hobby will suffice.

The Christian response that I have used in presenting seminars on stress is based around the idea that what was good enough for Jesus is probably not a bad panacea for us.

We read in the gospels that *'as Jesus grew he developed in mind and body and in favour with God and man'*. I like to think of this as a balanced way of living. We should take care of our bodies as well as feeding our minds, and we should maintain a social dimension within our community as well as a spiritual persona. If we can sustain this sort of balance in our lives, then I believe we are well on the way to finding a good coping mechanism for stress.

Recent surveys have revealed that people who sustain a spiritual activity weekly, that involves meeting like-minded people, live about seven years longer than people who don't. A major heart hospital in America reported that patients with a faith were 14 times more likely to recover after surgery than patients without a belief system.

This sense of belonging is so important, and carries with it responsibilities for us all. In some of the bigger churches that I have attended, maybe on holiday, I felt almost invisible, with people seeming to be so busy that the stranger in their midst is ignored. I have been in the counselling room with people who go to large churches just because they know they can remain anonymous but secretly hoping that someone might speak to them. Most people, even those with an anxiety complex, desperately want to feel connected to something or somebody.

Some other Milestones on Life's Journey.

A Look at The Roller Coaster Ride of Depression!

Ten years after my personal encounter with *stress becoming distress* I was working on the training group for B.T. presenting seminars on, among other things, stress. Isn't life funny! I heard my own story repeated many times with a wide variety of issues and illnesses, some resulting in death, from both organic disease and suicide.

When I did my counselling training at a GP surgery I became quite friendly with one of the GPs and we spent a lot of time together. He reckoned that 75 per cent of the people he saw in his surgery had medical or psychological problems inextricably linked to life-style.

Dorothy Rowe, the clinical psychologist, says as much and does not hesitate to link drug company profits to the need for doctors to prescribe pills for life style illnesses such as depression, anxiety and stress.

Depression *usually* tells you that that there is something wrong with the way you are living your life, or with the way that you make sense of the world. Pills can create a breathing space; they cannot turn a bad childhood into a good one or an abusive marriage into a fulfilled relationship or bring back a loved one who has died.

Labels are sometimes helpful for people with psychological problems but only if they are in the first place correct and secondly not written in permanent ink! I'm just as guilty about labels. I would willingly have worn a shirt top on my ride with the words, 'I'm not a real cyclist,' on it – a sort of 'get out' so that when the genuine article came racing by I would not have to compete or get into a conversation about the latest cycling gizmo advertised in some cycling magazine that I'd never heard of. Real cyclists wear really garish lycra body suits emblazoned with major company sponsorship labels. My clothes for the ride had little labels inside the collar with names such as 'St. Michael' and 'George' or 'Wilko'.

I well remember our son *having* to have trainers, tops and jeans with very specific label names. These symbols are designed to make statements about who we are and give us credibility within our peer group. Even the carrier bags in which the goods are carried are highly symbolic as we walk about the shopping mall. The marketing industry is, of course, ready to exploit this psychological hunger.

Depression is such a complex subject and renowned experts have written many, many volumes, but I have listened to sufferers for over fifteen years and share a few of my experiences.

Some therapists and doctors, needing to apply labels to patients who seem to be depressed, use some of the following terms: r*eactive,* which means some life event happened to cause the depression or *endogenous,* growing from within, or even *clinical depression* which means that it is so serious they suggest only specialist help can be of any use. However, I've yet to discover a true definition of clinical depression – and certainly some people with that label do not seem to know what it means! Another label might say *bi-polar or manic* which can be any of the above, but the depression swings from the very low activity level, or staying under the duvet syndrome, to being obsessive, highly verbose, and so active as to exhaust oneself and everyone around them.

Another type of depression is labelled *post-natal*, sometimes know as *baby blues*, which softens the sound of the problem, but not unfortunately the effects. This is very common, and can run in families, but whether that is through a genetic link or learnt behaviour is not really known yet. An interesting observation passed on to me from my daughter Emma, who has just had a baby, may be relevant here.

She discovered, through contact with health visitors, that new mums from an Asian background would spend six weeks after the birth of their baby almost exclusively at home, their only job during that time being to feed the baby; no cooking, cleaning, shopping or working – although feeding is of course work. She said that health visitors did not need to make appointments to visit, because mum and baby would be at home. I'm not too sure how this works if there are other young children about, but the sense of community seems a lot higher within that culture than within some others. This tradition seems very different from the expectations placed on most of the mums I have known. Although I have no evidence as to any link between the haste to get back to normal after giving birth and post-natal depression, the idea of this six-week ritual does suggest a more natural healthy rhythm.

Another label often used during the winter, especially after Christmas, is the *Seasonal Affective Disorder*, sometimes called S.A.D. There is plenty of evidence linking depression with cold dark days and lack of sunlight. The ideal prescription would be a week or two on a sunny beach, but that is not always possible. Even small amounts of exposure to a weak winter sun can help, along with fresh fruit, sensible eating and moderate exercise. One joyful bit of news here is that small quantities of chocolate, especially the dark variety, are known to improve depressive conditions, but I guess we all knew that anyway! If these measures on their own are not effective, then it is important to seek further help.

Graeme Obree, a Scot, recently wore the label *fastest cyclist in the world over one hour.* He now wears a different label; he is a *manic-depressive,* and has tried several times to end his life. He '*totally signed up to the theory that what we do as adults is driven by what we experienced as children*'. He was the son of a policeman, and never took a friend home in his entire school life. He felt isolated, socially excluded, suffered bullying and liked trees better than people. He said that winning cycle races was the only thing, apart from alcohol, that made him feel good.

The Samaritans report significant increases in people calling them after Christmas and suicides tend to be higher at that time of year. GPs see a lot of people in the mid-winter who will be categorised as T.A.T.T. (tired all the time). This is often a side effect of depression. It can be a serious condition and must be treated as such.

John Oxenham poetically links depression and choice, which I explored earlier in this book, and which depressed people may feel doesn't exist as far as they are concerned.

To every man there openeth
A way and ways and a way.
And the high soul climbs the high way
And the low soul gropes the low
And in between, on the misty flats
The rest drift to and fro.
But to every man there openeth
A high way and a low
And every man decideth the way his soul shall go.

Why are Some People Survivors While Others Remain Victims?

I am writing this whilst Lance Armstrong is winning his seventh Tour de France. I mentioned earlier what Armstrong believed about suffering. Here is a man who was diagnosed with testicular cancer with secondaries in his lungs and brain. I don't know if he has any faith structure in his life, but he chose to get back on his bike and become a world-beater. Why is it that some people seem to be survivors whilst others remain trapped in victim mode?

My own sister comes from the same mould as Armstrong. 'I've got too much to do to be ill,' I remember her saying ten years ago, after being diagnosed with Multiple Myeloma. She has proved all the cynics wrong.

A man I knew in my counselling work described his own condition as being like crucifixion addiction, because being metaphorically on the cross, horrible though that might be, was, he perceived, better than the alternatives. He got lots of support, money and sympathy as well as access to free therapy and so became used to not putting in place measures to help himself. He was by his own admission hooked on being a life-long victim.

Ellen Bass and Laura Davis, who wrote *The Courage to Heal*, the book that I believe has set the standard for working with adults abused as children, said this: 'People say time heals all wounds, and it's true to a certain extent. Time will dull some of the pain, but deep down healing doesn't happen unless you consciously choose it. Healing from child abuse takes years of commitment and dedication. But if you are willing to work hard, if you are determined to make lasting changes in your life, if you are able to find good resources and skilled support, you can not only heal but also thrive. We believe in miracles and hard work.'

I have used much of this material when working with adults who were abused as children and, painful though the memories might be, people do move on and live fulfilled lives. Ultimately clients have to make a choice, and if they make the decision to seek out a skilled helper then I guess that is sign that they want to change. The longest journey begins with one short step.

A Fatal Connection – Sometimes!

If anyone reading this is depressed or is living with someone who exhibits this type of psychological problem – I don't want to suggest they have not tried to 'escape the prison' as Dorothy Rowe the author and clinical psychologist, calls it. Neither do I suggest that it's easy to make headway against the relentless turmoil trapped within them. For some people I have known, at very close quarters, depression became a terminal illness! There is plenty of evidence that depression does run in families, and this might suggest a genetic link, but once again it would be foolish not to accept that this might also be learnt behaviour.

A recent headline in a national newspaper used the words, 'Come unto me, and I will give you lots of pills and make you happy.' The doctor writing the article said, 'Depression can strike anyone but while there is little doubt that there have been advances in treatment, it is doubtful whether the simultaneous medication of common unhappiness has been a blessing rather than a curse.' The article went on to say that old fashioned melancholia was, and still is, a severe condition, which deprives life of interest and meaning, manifests itself in agitation or sometimes stupor, can cause hallucinations and delusions and frequently leads, in a tenth or more cases, to suicide. About 5000 people a year take their own life in our country; about 75% of those are male. Chad Varah, the founder of the Samaritans was reported to have said, 'Quite often this is a long term solution to a short term problem.'

In the days when there were no specific treatments, care of such people was largely custodial. I can remember, as a teenager, visiting psychiatric wards in a hospital with the young people's group from the Baptist Church I attended. We took our guitars and led services on the wards. I can't remember if I cycled there but I can remember the seeming hopelessness of those people.

The Story of Reg and How There Isn't a Pill for Every Ill

Reg was one of my staff when I was working with B.T. He was afflicted by the memories of liberating prisoners of war from a concentration camp in 1945. He was about 18 years old when he was exposed to such horror that he never really recovered. I remember visiting him in a psychiatric ward in Darenth Park Hospital where he was routinely admitted for treatment using mainly electrical convulsive therapy (E.C.T.). He was a lovely man but never really escaped the prison he entered in 1945. He died at Darenth Grange in Carolyn's care during the 1980s.

However, in Western civilisation *most* human unhappiness is the consequence of the decisions people take about how to live their lives, or how they choose to perceive what has happened to them. Remember Frankl in the concentration camp? Unfortunately some forms of trauma are unavoidable in most societies, as was the case for Reg, and despite the best endeavours of himself, his friends and a host of medics he remained very ill for most of his life.

By prescribing medication for trauma or depression the doctor is implying, and the patient receiving, the message that the solution to unhappiness is a technical one, and not a matter of changing some aspect of his way of life. Some doctors like the message, because it both flatters their importance and draws many a consultation to a close, and some patients like it because deviation from the well-trodden path of misery is strenuous and frightening. If the tablets don't work, they prefer to believe that it is because the doctor hasn't found the right ones, rather than that the unhappiness from which they suffer is not susceptible to such painless manipulation.

Thus it is not difficult to see how anti-depressants, while useful in certain cases, may increase the sum of human misery by misleading people into not taking entirely possible and appropriate action for themselves.

This is where the talking therapies can really help because, while the spirits have been lifted by chemical intervention, there occur opportunities, within the right environment, to start looking at the issues causing the problem. Many doctors will suggest this dual approach; unfortunately, while the pills are readily available, access to psychological services is not. Whether rising prescriptions of antidepressants are caused by increasing unhappiness in the population at large, or the other way round, is a question difficult to answer. But in any individual case, the doctor will usually play safe: for medico-legal reasons, among others, he thinks it better that 99 should receive an unnecessary prescription than that one should fail to receive a necessary one.

I'm ***not*** saying that medication doesn't help to alleviate the symptoms of such conditions, but the need to address the underlying issues is the only real long-term answer, and sometimes if the trauma is so great then, as happened to Reg, there seems to be no solution.

One of the questions that people often ask in the counselling room is how they will know when they are better. Sometimes when working with clients when only a small number of sessions are available, it is the counsellor who would ask the client how life would be if the presenting problems miraculously disappeared overnight. Counsellors have to recognise the boundaries of their competence and are not qualified to advise on medication and whether a client should continue taking antidepressants. What seems to happen is that having started talking about the problems and taking medication, people often do feel a lot better. Most people don't want to be on medication so their natural inclination is to stop taking the pills. I always tell my clients that this should be decided in partnership with their medical advisor. However some clients take matters into their own hands and either stop or reduce their medication by personal choice. This is a really difficult area and no two people are the same. For someone going through a really messy divorce and is just not coping, then pills *and* talking therapies are probably appropriate for the duration of the process. However, for someone like my friend Reg, these can continue indefinitely.

Many of the people I work with ask whether it is possible to zap bad memories from their minds. In fact the opposite seems to be true; the more we try and bury difficult issues from the past the greater, the more powerful they become. It's almost as though hidden or suppressed memories are buried in the deep recesses of our minds just waiting to pop out and surprise us one day when the appropriate trigger is activated. As far as I am aware we don't have the ability to erase bad memories, but we can chose how we respond to them and decide how much they will affect our lives. Sometimes a client in the counselling room might say that the hurt is too great to live with, the scars are just too deep. I have a scar on my wrist and if I feel it is appropriate I might offer the client the chance to hear that while the scar is still clearly visible and I see it every day, the pain that caused the injury has gone away. *However I wouldn't tell them it was caused by a cycling accident!* For many people the pain of psychological injury is very intense; the discovery of their partner's affair or the drugs in their child's bedroom can throw their life into utter turmoil. Part of what some counsellors do is to try and instil hope in their clients, and for some, sowing the seed that the pain will diminish, while not denying that the scar tissue will remain, can be helpful. *Self-disclosure from a counsellor during a session is considered by some to be unprofessional but I feel that on rare occasions, where it will help the client, it can be justified.*

Most real cyclists are well endowed with scar tissue. If you have ever seen a high-speed cycle crash then it is not difficult to imagine how much skin, flesh and bone is left on the tarmac, and the injuries are sometimes very serious indeed. There is virtually no protection in the clothing worn, although helmets are now compulsory in most events. Although I have only reached speeds of 40 mph on very rare occasions, most of the top racing cyclists frequently exceeded 70 mph and there really isn't any way back if you fall off a bike at that speed.

An eminent psychologist from Canada lived in my village for a short while before she died. Hopefully there was no connection between the two events! She did take a fairly controversial approach to some disorders of the mind. She worked for over 50 years in the field of psychological problems and dreams, and had radio and television fame in Canada. When I asked her how she would work with someone suffering trauma from the past she said she would tell them to strip off, stand in front of a full-length mirror and see if they could see any scars resulting from the abuse. If they couldn't then she would tell them that all the problems were in their head and they, and they alone, had access and control over what went on in there. Knowing her as I did – she was a very caring lady – I'm sure the process was not quite as cut and dried as described, but she was pretty blunt about trauma.

In a funny sort of way she was saying quite similar things to what Victor Frankl, whom I referred to early on in this book, was saying. I know some of my colleagues at Sevenoaks Christian Counselling Service (S.C.C.S.) who visited this lady were quite shocked to hear this sort of treatment being suggested. However, given the choice of allowing clients to stay in victim mode for years, which is what some sections of the media claim counselling is about, or offering them this rather dramatic escape route, I know which one I would choose. This reminds me of the story about a client who had been seeing a psychotherapist for several years because of fears about monsters under her bed, this was causing severe sleep depravation. Eventually the client decided she was getting nowhere and stopped therapy. A few days later she happened to bump into an old friend in the supermarket and told him about her problem. Within a day she was cured. The therapist wanted to know how this had happened; the lady said that her friend was a practical sort of fellow and sawed the legs off her bed. Hooray for carpenters and common sense!

The barriers of the mind restricting people to live fulfilled lives are serious conditions whatever their causes. While some people are clearly victims wanting to become survivors there are others who seem to be locked into the 'poor me' culture.

In the sporting world most competitors are happy to acknowledge that on a given day they were beaten by a better man or woman, to shake hands and move on. Football club managers seem to be the obvious candidates for therapy; they nearly all want to blame either the referee or the state of the pitch or some extra terrestrial phenomena for yet another defeat. A classic case of denial! There does seem to be within our society a proliferation of the blame culture. There are adverts in the press and on television and radio encouraging us to sue everyone from local councils for potholes to burger bars for making us fat because we eat their fries. There are a significant number of people who simply refuse to accept responsibility for their plight or their actions and stay in victim mode seemingly for ever.

A Lonely Ride

A very recent survey has revealed that people suffering psychological problems have reduced life expectancy and more undiagnosed illnesses. Some of this, the report said, is caused by the medication, which can affect digestion and appetite. Reasons also given were that people suffering this affliction simply do not care about themselves enough and by their very nature the sufferer does not attract friends who could help.

During parts of the 1980s I felt very low. Although I was never depressed, it was a bit like the *end to end* ride – I was quite alone; but, in contrast to how I felt on the ride, I would have dearly liked someone riding with me. I do remember how important my golfing friends were. We played together a couple of times a month by queuing up at local courses at day break on Saturday mornings and I seem to recall that those few hours were my only real escape from the pressures of work, home and church. My friends were very important to me. I also recall that my bike was hanging up in the shed gathering cobwebs at the time! About ten years before that the only hint of dubious cycling pedigree had emerged when I cycled most Sunday mornings before going to church. My good friend David and I used to meet up and do about 20 miles. Perhaps I should have continued with that activity through the stressful times that came later.

One man whose bike did not gather much dust was Lance Armstrong; he writes very movingly about his journey during the cancer treatment. 'I got the cancer, I kept trying to ride though, and Bart and College, would go with me. Now they were the ones who could leave me in the dust, because I was so weak. One afternoon, when I was bald and thin and yellow from my third chemo cycle, I wanted to ride. I should have been in bed resting, but I insisted, so Bart and College went with me. We only went three or four miles when I started failing. I can't go on, I said, I gotta go back. College reached out and put a hand on my back and pushed me up that hill. I almost cried with the humiliation of it, but I was glad for the help. Those were the things we did for each other. What goes around comes around: we all need a push sometimes. If you're the one pushing others up the hill, there may come a day when you need a push, too. Maybe when you help someone, you're much closer to the top yourself.'

I have tried to explore the psychology, spirituality and physiology of journeys, my journey. By way of a summary I tell the following story.

Several years ago groups of learned cognitive behavioural psychologists, eminent Christian theologians and leading nutritional neurological scientists, were told to lock themselves away until they all agreed on statements that simple people like me could understand, about their respective disciplines. After many weeks and much heart searching they produced the following words of wisdom:
The behavioural psychologists said: *'Count your blessings name them one by one.'*
The theologians said: *'Jesus loves me this I know 'cause the Bible tells me so.'*
The nutritional neuro scientists said: *' A little of what you fancy does you good.*
I seem to remember my Granny telling me this when I was a lad!

Loss and Bereavement

I mentioned earlier that my friends, during the difficult times of the eighties, were very important to me. For two of them in particular, life events took their toll.

One of my friends died, quite suddenly; we all still miss his companionship, his humour, his loving and caring. For the other, whose wife died, life has found meaning again in a new relationship with a lovely lady whose husband died several years ago.

The issues around loss and bereavement are still very much the taboo of our generation within our culture. Approximately 650,000 people die in our country every year. It is thought that about 15 per cent of those deaths are early or unexpected and are rightly surrounded with anger, disbelief, blame, denial and a roller coaster of other emotions.

Insofar as life is a journey and all journeys have to end somewhere, there does seem to be an emerging theme that life should be extended at all costs. Even within the Christian tradition, where the promise of life everlasting is assured, death for the very old is often treated with great solemnity, most people wearing black and talking in hushed tones. I did say within our culture because for some in our land, with for example a Caribbean background, death is handled in a different way and is very much a celebration of the life lived and the life to come. Of course I am not saying that sadness shouldn't be a natural emotion of someone whose loved one or relation has died, whatever their age.

What I do find strange is that most doctors are reluctant to write *died of the diseases old age* as the cause of death for an elderly person. A lot of the people I have worked with believe that because pneumonia or heart failure or something similar was written on the death certificate, then some form of medical intervention could have saved them. I think that this just makes the grieving process more difficult.

I am familiar with most of the arguments about when it seems appropriate, or not, to cease medical intervention for someone who seems to have no quality of life. When you ask the question, 'Who wants to live for 100 years anyway?' the answer is, of course, 'Someone who is 99.' However I believe our modern hospice movement, certainly the one closest to my heart, has got it about right in what is appropriate treatment for the very sick. I am *not* suggesting that because The Ellenor hospice organisation is based on Christian principles it necessarily has a monopoly in what is perceived as excellence in care of the terminally ill. For example, given the choice of going to a *good* Christian who happens to be dentist, or a *good* dentist who happens to be a Christian, I know whom I would choose. Sometimes, as I believe is the case for The Ellenor Foundation, the Christian option is the best.

With the advance in stem cell research there exists the possibility of extending life way beyond what we now regard as a natural cycle. The debate about living wills, cell regeneration and euthanasia will extend long after this writer has fallen off his bike for the last time.

Words from the third chapter of Ecclesiastes in the Old Testament have lost none of their relevance for our generation. If you have recently lost a loved one try reading the words slowly and see how relevant they may be to your situation. Made famous in the 1960s, by the The Byrds in a pop song we are reminded that '*there is a time for everything, and a season for every activity under heaven, a time to be born and a time to die, a time to plant and a time to uproot, a time to kill and a time to heal, a time to tear down and a time to build, a time to weep and a time to laugh, a time to mourn and a time to dance, a time to scatter stones and a time to gather them, a time to embrace and a time to refrain, a time to search and a time to give up, a time to keep and a time to throw away, a time to tear and a time to mend, a time to be silent and a time to speak, a time to love and a time to hate, a time for war and a time for peace'*. These words are often used at funerals and I do believe they make a lot more sense than some of the other liturgy that is supposed to bring comfort to those who mourn.

I so wish that more Churches would take a lead in the whole area of death, bereavement and grief. Some evangelicals seem to almost delight in making sure that non-believers are acquainted with the concept of eternal damnation. I have attended a funeral where we were reminded that it was not only in the crematorium where there will be flames! The Anglicans and Catholics continue to hatch, match, and dispatch with gay abandon. However I know of at least one priest who made it her mission to follow up families of those she had buried, to counsel, support and encourage them; and of another priest who did not think it appropriate even to mix with the family after the funeral service. I wonder what Jesus would do!

If you know the tune of 'Onward Christian Soldiers' try using these words to the first two lines:

Like a mighty tortoise moves the Church of God,
Brothers we are treading where we've always trod.

The Church in our land has to change or it will die. I remember the comment from one quite staid, loyal and seemingly devout parishioner of the Anglican tradition when guitars were played during a service: ' If Jesus could hear that racket he would turn over in his grave.'

I think the Vicar invited her to the next Alpha course.

I recall another story from the non-conformist tradition when a church was selecting a new minister. One potential candidate offered to move the church *forward* to places hitherto unimagined, using all the latest communication skills. The other said he would take the church *back* 2000 years and introduce its members to the core beliefs of the faith. I'm not sure whom they picked, but part of not wanting to change is about feelings of loss. The familiar can be safe to some, whilst the unfamiliar can be quite threatening to others. Within Anglican Churches some communicants sense feelings of loss because the 1662 prayer book is no longer used. It connects them with the past, they feel that an old friend has died. In a way I can almost understand the logic of the non-conformist ministers mentioned above in their polarised views about change. I do struggle with the notion of wanting to keep things locked into an era created just a few hundred years ago, whether it be the liturgy or the furniture, unless we are fully paid up members of the local historical society and not the living Christian church. I love history and I love old buildings, but in so far as we have provided heating and sound amplification and better lighting in most of our churches why do we want to keep hold of other aspects that make the very act of worship so uninviting?

If Armageddon has not arrived by that time I can just imagine my great great grandchildren complaining about having to sing those boring old Graham Kendrick songs. 'Can't we sing something modern and relevant?' they will be saying. However I hope the Kyrie Eleison (Lord, have mercy) would have survived the passage of time; that does seem to have an enduring resonance.

The words that I hear over and over again from people who have lost their mate is, 'I am so lonely,' and for many people who suffer the loss of their partner, the desire to ride in tandem again rather than being solo is compelling. There is plenty of evidence to suggest that this a normal healthy approach. This does not, of course, mean that the previous relationship was unhappy or unfulfilled. It could be that it was so good that there exists a strong desire to try and recapture some of it. *Dying of a broken heart* is another cause of death unlikely to be used by a doctor in recording why somebody may have died. There are countless examples of a surviving spouse dying very soon after the loss of their mate. This points very clearly to a link between our emotions and our physical well being. The physiological research would show that the immune system shut down, the real answer, I believe, is that the surviving partner just lost the will to live.

In my work as a bereavement counsellor there tended to be a stronger desire from men to find a new mate than from women. It would appear that women seem to cope better on their own. The other factor affecting this is that women on average live about 8 years longer than men. Old peoples homes and Age Concern meetings reflect a proportion of about one man to seven women over the age of 75 years. This is great news for the men who do have the longevity gene!

For others the pain of the loss can be so great that the thought of replacing the person who has died is not an option. It is the word *replace* that does cause some problems for those who do hitch up again. They will say that quite often it is seen as that, but in reality you cannot replace someone who has died. That would be a denial of the uniqueness of each individual.

So for my two friends mentioned earlier the journey has continued, but along different highways.

Of all the books I have read on the subject of loss, C.S. Lewis in *A Grief Observed* seems best to capture the deep feelings that engulf those who grieve. He, as it were, becomes an observer of himself and reflects on his own grief after his wife died. His story is beautifully portrayed by Anthony Hopkins in the film *Shadowlands*.

Lewis challenges God, calling it 'the monkey trick of a spiteful imbecile, a mean joke' when asking why God allowed Beethoven to go deaf. 'Oh my dear, my dear, come back for one moment and drive that miserable phantom away. Oh God, God, why did you take such trouble to force this creature out of its shell if it is now doomed to crawl back, to be sucked back into it?' I guess that in these words he was talking about himself, because he married late in life and was resigned at one stage to being a bachelor, until he fell in love. He felt that his marriage was too perfect to last. He describes how it felt as though he was at a sherry-party and just as he was getting into a real conversation with a guest, the hostess separated them. How, just as God saw two of his creatures happy, he stopped it. 'None of that here,' was what Lewis felt God was saying.

C.S. Lewis was also positive about his faith and his loss as well; he reasoned that, perhaps God said, 'Good, you have mastered that exercise, I am very pleased with it, now you are ready to go on to next.' He also picks up the theme of riding in tandem; he describes marriage as a healing between the sexes, jointly the two becoming fully human; in the image of God created He *them*. Then one or other dies, and of this Lewis writes, 'We think of this as love cut short; like a dance stopped in mid career or a flower with its head unluckily snapped off.' However he sees separation as part of the journey. As marriage follows courtship as autumn follows summer. It is not, he says, a truncation of the process but one of its phases; not the interruption of the dance but the next figure.

Abuse

Drug Abuse

Psychological and emotional, as well as physical and spiritual abuse, is quite often a common factor in people who seek help.

The world of professional cycling has tried harder than most to rid itself of drug abuse. It was rampant for many years. Tommy Simpson, perhaps the greatest ever cyclist from these shores, with Chris Boardman and Graeme Obree coming close second, died on the Tour de France he so desperately wanted to win. In 1965 at the age of 28 he was world champion and voted BBC Sports Personality of the Year. Two years later, and knowing that was probably his best and last chance to win the Tour de France, he pushed himself beyond the limits of human endurance. Video footage of his final moments, include those now infamous words to his coach as he was dying: 'Put me back on the bloody bike.' It was make or break and he broke.

During the Second World War soldiers of all sides were given over 70 million amphetamines to stifle fatigue and pain under a mental blanket of aggression and stamina. It didn't take the sports people of the world long to get in line for this stuff and the cyclists were at the front of the queue.

Jacques Anquetil, five times winner of the Tour de France in the Sixties, was quoted as saying, 'Only an imbecile imagines that a professional cyclist who rides 235 days a year can hold himself together without stimulants.' Tommy Simpson's choice was not whether to take speed, but how much and what brand.

The debate about performance-enhancing drugs in sport will endure. I grew up when the East Europeans used to win all the athletic medals for strength events. The women especially were enormous, having been pumped up with drugs. Everybody in sport knew it was going on. At the other end of the scale young female gymnasts had their physical development inhibited to keep them small and supple. The present focus is now on the Chinese where some remarkable performances are emerging and likely to cause problems in the next Olympics which they are to host.

I took drugs on my ride. Shock, horror! Well, it depends what you mean by drugs. When I was cold I drank hot tea or coffee, both contain caffeine, a well-known stimulant. I ate Kendal mint cake when I needed an energy boost, or chewed a dried banana when I was tired. These products, at present, are permitted although caffeine was once on the banned list. Who is to say what is OK and what is not? The old argument about only eating what is natural is dead and buried, because virtually everything we eat today is manufactured or refined somewhere along the production line, even if the seed wasn't genetically modified.

We all have limits – physical, emotional, spiritual and intellectual To try and exceed these in unnatural ways by whatever means will eventually take its toll.

Although performance-enhancing *drugs* seem to be in decline in the world of cycling, other processes are being used. In the past 12 months at least eight world-class cyclists have died in mysterious circumstances. This very high proportion of deaths, compared to other sports, seems to suggest that something is going on, and the finger of suspicion is pointing towards a process that thickens the blood and enables the muscles to extract more oxygen.

Psychological Abuse

This type of abuse seems far more common than physical or sexual abuse for children, who often become the casualties in the war between their parents. Children are very sensitive to the behaviour of their parents and will often model what they see. Many teenagers cannot wait to flee the nest to escape the difficulties at home. The females so often seem to end up in a relationship with a man who, far from rescuing the woman, simply exacerbates the problem. The male from the dysfunctional family has learnt from a poor role model and probably takes that learnt behaviour into his relationship, so perpetuating another unhealthy cycle. Unfortunately violence often follows hard on the heels of the psychological abuse and the scars become visible. Domestic abuse in our land is increasing at an alarming rate, and is often linked to alcohol or drugs.

Sometimes this type of abuse works against the man. It is not uncommon for a man to marry a woman who seems to provide a mother figure. As the relationship develops, especially if children arrive, the man can be feel usurped and become almost child-like.

When working with couples, it is thought that the relationship dynamics within the counselling room are often indicative of what goes on within the home and family. Quite often I might see a dominant woman who shows nothing but contempt for her husband. '*Apart from being useless in bed, and unable to even put a shelf up, you don't earn enough, can't make decisions, and by the way you're a lousy driver and lack ambition,'* are words that come to mind. Our archetypal *hunter-gatherer* has just crept back into his cave to lick his wounds. Abuse isn't all one way!!

I believe it was one of the Marx Brothers who said it was little wonder he was a screwed up adult because one of his parents was a woman and one of them was a man!

Issues with couples often boil down to needs and wants. They agree that a new car is *required;* he *wants* the top of the range with go-faster stripes, alloy wheels, heated seats, soft top and a turbo charger; but all she *needs* is a safe reliable means of transport for the school run. They might agree that the family *requires* a holiday. She *wants* to go to Florida on a fly- drive with five days at Disney World, he reckons a self catering bargain chalet at Butlins is all they really *need.*

Communication, or rather the lack of it, is another of the big issues at the heart of relationship problems and can be another string in the bow of the psychological abuser. We live in an age where we have the ability to establish instant contact with family and friends no matter where they are on the planet. However time and time again I hear couples saying that they don't talk to each other. Texting and E mails are a poor substitute for face to face dialogue. I remember Cliff Richard having a hit song called, 'We don't talk anymore'. Couples now say, 'We don't text anymore' after having already stopped talking, sending faxes and exchanging E mails. Some of the families I have worked with consider sending text messages as the primary means of communication. Mobile phones do of course have a rightful place in our world and are here to stay in one form or another. They can even be a way of initiating new friendships, but on their own will not sustain a meaningful relationship, because communication and real relationships are about a lot more than words. '*But I did tell you – didn't you get my text – I bet you didn't even have it switched on, or have you lost it again – you're hopeless?*' is not an untypical comment from a parent to a child of the 21st century. **For the psychological well being of the people most important in your life don't please buy them a 3G mobile as a substitute for that other most precious gift you can give them: an hour or two of your undivided attention. This is not *just* about spending time with children, for older people living on their own, the chance to just sit and talk to another human being, is powerful medicine indeed.**

Many of the above behavioural traits are rooted in the traditions of the families in which the couple were nurtured as children. Quite often it is not about rights and wrongs but about an understanding of why the couple thinks and behaves in the way they do.

Philip Larkin wrote this; I've changed some words to render the poem decent.

They muck you up, your mum and dad.
They may not mean to, but they do.
They fill you with the faults they had,
And add some extra, just for you.
But they were mucked up in their turn,
By fools in old-style hats and coats,
Who half the time were soppy-stern
And half at one another's throats.
Man hands on misery to man,
It deepens like a coastal shelf.
Get out early as you can,
And don't have kids yourself.

This is not a personal issue for me but I think Larkin captures well the recurring themes within the counselling room.

Spiritual Abuse

I've worked with Christian couples where the man will sit in the counselling room and demand that his wife be submissive and subject to his authority. The apostle Paul could never have known how much trouble he would cause! The idea of love, respect and compassion being part of the dynamics within the relationship seems a distant concept.

These messages, I regret to say, are also delivered from many a pulpit and the recipients are further crushed. I have no hesitation in calling this spiritual abuse.

I have experienced this on my journey. I recognise the description by Johnson and Van Vonderen in their book, *The Subtle Power of Spiritual Abuse*. They describe *power posturing* where leaders spend a lot of time focused on their own authority and reminding others of it. This is necessary because their spiritual authority isn't real – based on genuine Godly character -- it is *postured*. To restore some balance to this issue, I have also worked and worshipped with some who were clearly Christ – like.

Some of the most difficult sessions I've had on my counselling journey have been with clients who say they have been healed in church the previous Sunday. They still feel depressed, anxious, angry, lost, dirty, afflicted with addiction, or whatever it was they felt before, but they have been pronounced healed. When they question this with their minister, vicar or elders, they are often told that there must be still more undisclosed sins from the past. We will spend the counselling hour trying to make sense of all this. I often feel quite angry after sessions like this because clients seem overwhelmed, not by the love of Christ, but by dogma and doctrine.

I remember one client who really could not cope with this and went from her evangelical church to a middle of the road Anglican. It was here that she was introduced to the prayer of humble access, which are words used before the communion service. She became distressed all over again having to say every week that *she was not worthy even to pick up the crumbs from under God's table.* Counsellors can learn a lot from their clients. I had for example, never really thought about those words before. We decided in the counselling room that we were both worthy because of what Christ had done on the cross. I know that some of my theological friends disagree with me, but what's new about that? So along with my client I stopped using those words, I simply don't believe them to be helpful. I suppose that wording is a slight improvement on the words used in The Book of Common Prayer 1662 edition. Here we are told that: *we kindle God's wrath against us; we provoke him to plague us with divers diseases, and sundry kinds of death.'* That is said before we declare ourselves *as miserable sinners.* Truly great medicine for any one predisposed towards depression! However I never was *a miserable* sinner, some of it was great fun! Do I sense excommunication coming on? This is not intended as a criticism of Christianity but of personal interpretation. It was William Temple who said, 'It's not that Christianity has been tried and found wanting, it is that Christianity has been found difficult and not tried.' I do try, but I see no harm in questioning and even challenging some of the established dogma and doctrine.

There does seem to exist a vast gulf within the Christian tradition about interpreting scripture and its meaning for our generation.

My own understanding in relating to how we can make sense of the conflict between the extremes of our faith structure goes like this: The Bible is the inspired word of God but it is like a musical score. Even where the notes are clearly written on the stave, different musicians and conductors will interpret those notes in different ways. Also even during the lifetime of the musician, interpretation of any given score may also change. Extending the musical analogy a little more, a good choir needs voices of all tones and shapes. Similarly the strength of our faith, I believe, rests partly in its diversity and I long for the day when the world hears the harmony and not the discord.

I know for some that these issues are as simple as freewheeling and quote the scripture to support their stance, but for me I find these matters a hard uphill painful slog in heavy mist. Can I hear my theological friends beating a path to my door again? I think I need to get on my bike quickly, not forgetting my helmet of course; perhaps a breastplate, sword, belt, shoes and shield might also come in handy. If this bit doesn't make sense, read Ephesians chapter 6.

I am Just Not Good Enough For This.

Low self-esteem, as it is often referred to, is one of the most prominent characteristics that people present within the counselling room. I certainly had serious doubts about my own ability to complete the ride; self-belief was not overflowing!

If we can be set free from those destructive patterns of behaviour and learn to punch the air, even if only with one fist, then we can be free indeed.

How do therapists work with someone who says, 'I'm useless; nobody would miss me if I died tonight ?'

Victor Frankl talks about this in his book. He would ask a client hinting at ending their life, 'What is it that stops you from committing suicide?' Most people have some reason and that can be a good starting point.

Another therapist tells the story of a lady who wanted to die; she had no family, no purpose for living. The therapist knew that she was a churchgoer, but the lady didn't like the modern hymns and liturgy and said, 'Nobody would miss me,' several times during the session. What the therapist also noticed was a collection of African violets in the lady's kitchen. He suggested she might like to give him a cutting. She readily agreed, and from this developed an idea. The lady now presents everyone in her church with a healthy plant on their birthday as well as giving a plant to people who have suffered the loss of a loved one. She has found her ministry and a purpose for living through a flowerpot.

I remember one client, who told me she was broken and useless. I told her a story. It was about two people who every day had to walk through a garden down to a river to collect water to fill a tub. One person was fast and had a posh new container and made lots of journeys and soon filled the tub. The other person was slower and had a broken container that leaked and took a long time to complete the task. After several months someone noticed lots of pretty flowers growing alongside the path. They discovered that the drips from the broken container carried by the slow person had given life to these plants. We don't have to be perfect to be of value!

I am reasonably confident that despite a great amount of help from friends, this book will contain sOmE eRrors. This is because all us who are not perfect can identify with it. For everyone else I am really sorry and seek your forgiveness.

During my time as a manager with B.T. I had to conduct annual appraisements of my staff. For several years I gave them blank copies of the reports and invited them to assess themselves. It was very rare to find anybody who marked themselves higher than my perception of their performance. It certainly made life easy for me in carrying out an exercise most managers used to dread!

Part of my counselling work is with staff from local companies and I might encourage them to write their C.V. Not the true one but the one they might aspire to; a sort of wish list of potential. It's amazing what emerges if you give someone the space to write or talk about themselves in a non-judgmental, empathic environment.

Another simple process when working with people presenting with low self worth might be to ask them how tall they are, and then asking them how tall they *feel*. Quite often somebody *feeling* low will actually walk into the counselling room with their head and shoulders held low and slump into the chair. The process that works for some clients goes something like this: if they say they *feel* four foot nothing then I ask, 'What would it take to feel four foot and half an inch.' Once, one client looked up and said, 'If there was a lock on the toilet door.' She had several children and even privacy in the smallest room in the house was denied her by her partner's intransigence about fitting a bolt.

The following week she did come back feeling four foot and half an inch!!

Rob Parsons who heads up the organisation *Care for the Family* says in his book *The Sixty Minute Marriage* 'It is often a thousand little things that cause the trouble in relationships.'

Couples often ask me, 'What are the main issues that bring people like us to see a counsellor?' Relate, the organisation delivering most of the couples' therapy in

England say that the top two subjects are money or finance – usually where the man cannot deliver all that the woman wants – and sex – usually where the woman cannot deliver all that the man wants – but not always that way round! However I do not entirely agree with Relate. I would say that dishwashers and washing machines have a lot to answer for as well. I've lost count of the number of sessions I've spent listening to couples argue about how to load a dishwasher. Of course it is a well-known fact that the male of the species has a greater ability when it comes to spatial awareness. However it is usually the female of the species who has to empty the appliance and rewash all the crocks that didn't come clean because they were crammed in too close together. When it comes to washing machines I have become an expert on what you can and cannot wash together. A typical exchange might be: 'My mother would never have dreamt of washing towels with anything else.' 'Well, my mother always did and I didn't catch anything.' When it comes to temperature settings then a whole new debate ensues. 'Do you realise how much it costs to heat water to 80 degrees?' 'Well, if you wash them at 50 degrees then they don't come clean.' Fortunately for the clients, this counsellor does not give advice!

Inside the counselling rooms at S.C.C.S. we have trays of pebbles, along with many other creative materials. It might seem appropriate to offer some clients the chance to select some stones from the collection, to represent their family or workplace. It is fascinating to watch how carefully some clients select the objects. The stone that represents a client may be very small and badly shaped; perhaps their partner or parent might be large and round and perfectly formed. *Where* the stone is placed on the tray is also significant. Quite often the clients stone may be on the edge and the rest close together in the middle.

Having constructed this model, it might be suggested that the client choose a stone more appropriate to what they would *like* to be, and perhaps move closer or maybe further away from the others. One of my colleagues told me that her client attached such significance to the model that at the end of the session she asked whether the tray could be carefully put away so that it would remain intact until she returned the following week. The process becomes effective when the client begins to identify ways of changing from the misshapen chipped pebble on the edge of the tray to the rounded complete stone in the middle and this is usually done by a series of small steps. I love the story of the little boy who asked a famous sculptor how he sculpted a horse from a solid block of granite. 'Well lad, I just chip away all the bits that don't look like a horse,' was the artists reply.

The roots for most of the feelings of low self-esteem are developed early on in life, perhaps from poor parenting. So often, as I explored in the chapter on abuse, even if these are successfully dealt with, entering into an abusive relationship can re-ignite all those feelings of worthlessness. Abuse is not just seen on the surface; it can be buried deep within, but the scars are there just the same.

I had an interesting light-hearted example of this just recently. I was sitting at a table in our church hall for a social meal along with about 60 other people. There were about eight people on my table and I was sitting at the end. A couple of ladies close by were talking about what sort of knitting stitch to use on a garment or some other subject which seemed to exclude me, so I picked up a book I was reading. I was immediately taken to task by one of the ladies who declared, 'My mother would not approve of reading at the table.' After establishing that her mother had died many years before, the debate shifted from knitting to behavioural traits and why we say and do what we do – a topic of far more interest than knitting patterns – at least to me. The voices from our past can be a great comfort but they can also be suffocating. We do have a choice as to which ones to heed and which to ignore.

A Little Theory From Another Trick Cyclist!

It was John Bowlby, just after the Second World War, who developed the notion of Attachment Theory. He was asked by the United Nations World Health Organisation to study the effects of mother-child separation in early life. What he concluded was that it is essential for mental health that the infant and young child should experience a warm, intimate and continuous relationship with his mother or a permanent mother-substitute in which both find satisfaction and enjoyment.

The researchers discovered that babies separated from their mothers showed signs of distress. They observed that there are certain demonstrable phases that each child passes through and that the pre-school years, especially the period from 6 months to 3 years, are critical.

Why is this you might ask? One of the reasons why early childhood experiences are so important for later life is that the developing child internalises his experiences as they learn their first lessons about what life is like and what to expect from other people. If those adults closest to the child, and the parents' role is critically important here, respond in a cold, careless or inconsistent way to the child's needs, then the child is likely to grow up expecting those around him or her to be unreliable and untrustworthy.

Dr. Eric Berne the founder of Transactional Analysis in the 1950s also recognised the power of the parental messages in his theory. He recognised three states, namely parent adult and child, that we all embrace. It is as though as a little child we record all the messages delivered by our parents on a tape, and replay them later in life. If the messages are consistent and genuine then that is what we replay. If they are confused or violent and unloving then that is what as a child we internalise, and when we hit the replay button that is what usually emerges.

Admitting That Sometimes it Really Hurts, and in More Than One Place! A Brief Look at Emotions.

Another story from Rob Parsons' book *The Sixty Minute Marriage*, tells the tale of the little boy at the circus who sees the clown laughing and joking in the circus ring, but when the child goes backstage and the mask comes off the clown, the little boy sees sadness and tears.

I guess we all wear the odd mask depending on who we are with. If you can find the right person to be with, try removing the mask now and again. Women are better at this than men, certainly within our culture. We seem to be better at watching *Friends* on television than making them in real life.

There was quite an amazing difference between the clients I worked with in the GP surgery and most of those I see in Sevenoaks at S.C.C.S. The GP practice claimed to have the highest morbidity rate in the area, whereas Sevenoaks, just a few miles up the road has one of the highest densities of high-income earners in the south east of England. My counselling supervisor once asked me to describe a particular client in Sevenoaks. I settled on the phrase 'Laura Ashley, 4 wheel drive'. 'Ah yes' she said, 'I see'. *Supervision is mandatory for all counsellors associated with the regulatory authority, but does not compromise client confidentiality.* Most of the people I saw in the surgery would perhaps be 'Matalan, 3 wheel Reliant Robin'. The joy for me is that both sets of people were created in the image of God and had access to psychological services in their moments of need.

There was a vast gulf in the ability of the two types of people to express their feelings. The folk at the surgery had a somewhat limited vocabulary but left me in no doubt about how they were feeling.

The people in Sevenoaks have, generally, a far wider vocabulary but some find it more difficult to express their feelings. Admitting that it hurts is alien to some sections of our community.

How often does a conversation with a friend begin, 'How are you?' and our conditioned response is usually, 'Fine thanks.' Wouldn't life be better if we responded with the truth? I know it's very naughty but quite often when one of those really polite people from India ring to ask you to change your phone supplier, my response to their 'How are you today Mr Forman?' is to say that I have a terminal illness, This is usually followed by a few moments of silence and then they ask me if I am likely to be making any long distance calls in the near future! Although I don't want to buy their product it is really interesting to allow them to talk about their way of life, their family and interests, These people are highly trained and well qualified but seem unable or unwilling to actually hear what you are telling them. How would you respond if someone told you that they were dying?

A little tip worth remembering: about 80% of communication is non verbal, so next time someone says, 'Oh I'm OK,' or whatever, in their reply to your, 'How are you question?' see if you can read anything more into those few words. Notice the tone of voice and body language; watch the face, eye contact, speed of response. What words were emphasised? All of these can be clues as to what is really going on. If you find this sort of thing interesting, and can listen a little better than you can talk, then pursue it with some reading or training on listening skills. A new vocation might be right around the corner!

A GP in Sevenoaks was commenting on the lack of emotional literacy among some of his patients. 'They have loads of money but seem unable to express feelings.' he said and added that they have just as many problems as the rest of society, it's just that they have longer drives.

I understand from a friend who is a head teacher that a curriculum activity is being considered called EQ (emotional quotient). The idea is to educate children in understanding feelings.

What is appropriate within our culture in terms of expressing anger, grief, frustration, joy....? Sometimes big boys do cry and actually it's OK. I remember Paul Gascoigne, affectionately known as Gazza, the England footballer, crying after being yellow – carded and realising that he might miss a World Cup final. Perhaps we need more role models who express feelings in an appropriate way, though our culture might resist this!

I attended a meeting with the head of care at an ex-armed-services residential unit for soldiers suffering from trauma. He asked me to guess the average age of the inmates. I was way out, having suggested ex-Falklands, ex-Gulf, ex-Afghanistan, perhaps even Northern Ireland. They were, in fact, ex-World War Two soldiers: men whose wives had recently died, who were in their eighties and nineties, and were now living on their own. All the memories of the war had come flooding back into the vacuum created by their bereavement. They had either been unwilling or unable to tell their story for over fifty years. I know Carolyn has experienced this phenomenon in her work with the dying.

The stiff upper lip is alive and well and in a home near you today!

After giving a talk in our village about the *end to end* ride it was good to get some feedback suggesting that we did convey the agony as well as the ecstasy of the journey.

Behaviour

An interesting observation on the ride was the behaviour of other road users. I used to do a bit of canoeing and a sort of unwritten rule of the water was that power gave way to sail and sail gave way to paddle and paddle gave way to swim.

Cyclists used to have some rights but even in sleepy Meopham it's every man for himself on the roads. There was a marked contrast in road manners almost directly related to the distance north we travelled. Certainly in Scotland I felt far safer cycling than in Kent. Whether this is borne out statistically I don't know, but people seemed friendlier, the pace of life slower and the rat race a distant memory. Carolyn noticed that children and babies were left in pushchairs outside shops in the north of Scotland.

How refreshing that within the cycling world people do stop and chat and almost always check if things are OK and ask if you have any problems with the bike.

Even in the Tour de France a code of behaviour exists that is not seen in many other sports today. Cyclists will not seek to gain an advantage if the leader has a puncture or is involved in an accident. They do seem to have made giant strides to try and rid the sport of performance-enhancing drugs, at least for a while, to the extent of even banning antihistamine for insect bites; perhaps that's taking things a bit too far. Or should that be a bite too far!

I do recognise that anger management is a highly marketable product here in the South. I have personal experience of road rage, office rage, trolley rage in the local supermarkets, lane rage in the swimming pool and Zimmer rage ... very painful ... in a home for the elderly. I even had a bit of pew rage in the local Church when I sat in the wrong place, and fairway rage on the golf course is approaching epidemic proportions.

Tennyson captured the North /South divide in these words:

Bright and fierce and fickle is the South, dark and true and tender is the North.

A Little Exercise Can Go a Long Way

There is overwhelming evidence that even moderate forms of exercise can have a significant effect in redressing the psychological problems of depression, anxiety and self-destructive addiction phobias as well as low self worth. Drinking alcohol to excess on a regular basis and binge drinking and eating are very effective ways of coping in the short term for a number of people. Unfortunately they have some added hidden extras that include broken relationships, debt, deeper depression, loss of libido, obesity, and death to name just a few! Certainly what we eat and drink does affect the way we cope with any form of illness, but do remember the words of Paul the Apostle, '*Moderation in all things*'. My own revised version is slightly different, 'M*oderation in all things, especially moderation*'.

A recent report issued jointly by the Government's chief medical advisor and the Food Standards Agency suggests that, for the first time since records began, life expectancy has reduced. This has been caused by poor diet, creating obesity in the young and the not so young, as well as lack of exercise in all age groups. These findings are supported in the British Cohort Studies from the Centre for Longitudinal Studies Institute of Education at the University of London. They are following the lives of all the people born in a specific week during 1946,1958, and 1970. In the first study 5,362 people have been tracked, in the second17,414 and in the third in 1970, 17,198 people have been surveyed at age 2,5,10,13,21,26 and 30. The surveys will continue throughout the lives of the all the people born in those specific weeks. Carolyn and I have followed the findings with close interest because our eldest daughter was one of those involved in 1970 study.

There are similar battles with food as there are with prescribed drugs, where very powerful commercial lobbying is overwhelming the government messages on sensible eating. For example one 500ml bottle of Coke contains about 10 teaspoons of sugar.

The NHS spends about £880 per person a year treating sick people but its budget for health promotion is only £2.20. The message about consumption of fat has produced some good results and raised public awareness. A statement from the Department of Health suggests that once the campaign on reduction of salt is over then the sugar war will begin. Will there be any fun left in eating, I ask myself? Seriously though, the Sugar Bureau encourages us to consume sugar to replenish lost energy; they ask supermarkets to stack their products near the checkouts, and buy advertising space in prime time children's television. When we are living a sedentary lifestyle, we simply don't burn enough calories to justify their claims, unless you are cycling from Land's End to John O' Groats when you will definitely be in energy deficit!

There is a link between obesity and depression in the way that both dieting and antidepressants are effective in the providing a short-term fix to a specific problem. Diets can generate weight loss, but subsequently if intake exceeds output, then it's not rocket science to realise that weight will increase. This is why some people talk about the yo-yo effect of weight loss and weight gain. The only real answer, as with depression is, to address some lifestyle issues and make some choices and changes. I do of course recognise that, as with depression, where not everybody can be fixed with short term psychological and medical interventions, then for some people control of body weight and fitness can be very difficult due to underlying medical conditions.

The balance between eating and activity is so important, especially for our children, where recent research is suggesting that major problems with obesity and type 2 diabetes are looming.

The doctor's prescription for a little exercise, after getting yourself checked over first, might be to exercise 3 times a week to a point at which you are out of breath but still able to talk. Aim for about 20 minutes each time of whatever you choose – fast walking, cycling, swimming, aqua aerobics, playing tennis, jogging – but watch your joints. Choose whatever suits you. Don't forget to get yourself checked over by your medic and start slowly. Warm up first and keep the fluid intake high, avoiding alcohol or caffeine, which can act as diuretics and cause dehydration.

Our bodies were designed to be exercised. Listen to your body, if you can't bear to look at it. What is it saying to you? It really likes to be put through its paces, and if your genetic mapping tells you that competitive sport, trainers and track suits is not what you do, that's OK; just try using the stairs instead of the escalator or lift at the shopping mall. When visiting the supermarket try parking as far away from the entrance as you can; there is always more space there as well. You can even do a little weight training at the same time by carrying your bags back to the car. Have one bag in each hand and extend your arms out sideways slowly and then hold and lower. Don't worry about what people might think; they are probably paying £300 a year for gym membership to do the same exercise!

There are some hidden extras here as well. Apart from the psychological feelings of well being, exercise will help you sleep better, improve your cardio-vascular function, make you less susceptible to disease and, if the exercise is aerobic, will make your bones denser and less liable to fracture. If you combine some of this with sensible eating, you might even lose a bit of weight and then you wouldn't need to pump your bicycle tyres up so hard!

In America obesity and health concerns about physical fitness are reaching epidemic proportions. A team of architects have created one solution. They are now designing buildings in which the stairways are wide, bright and sweeping, and the lifts – or elevators, as our American cousins call them are small, dark and dingy. They are placing car parks for new office developments several hundred yards away from the building, and the response from most of the workers has been very positive. They have of course, considered the needs of those who through disability are unable to walk up stairs.

Postscript

There were several moments on the ride when I felt especially buoyant. Crossing the border into Scotland was one; another was seeing a sign post with John O' Groats on it, albeit 109 miles distant; and a third was having a riding companion, when Richard my son in law joined me for a day. But the greatest feeling was seeing the Orkney Islands from the top of Wrath Hill in Caithness, and knowing that John O' Groats was nestling on the coast just a few miles down the road. Actually arriving at the end was in a strange sort of way almost an anti -climax. The weather on the last day was simply perfect, and the views stunning. We booked the camper van into the site that was perched just about on the beach, and after the customary shower and mug of tea we wrote nearly 70 postcards to the friends who had sponsored the ride. Carolyn sent a text message to all our mobile phone friends who had supported us throughout the journey, and within a couple of hours every one had replied.

We had planned a holiday for a few days after successful completion of the ride, and did get over to the West Coast of Scotland at The Kyle of Lochalsh.

We booked into a Bed and Breakfast with the idea of crossing over to the Isle of Skye the following day. However the weather broke and so we settled for the cruise around the bay, which we had done the previous evening, as our Skye experience. We headed off to Northumbria and camped near Lindisfarne. We stayed for a couple of nights and cycled across the causeway to Holy Island.

The idea of having a holiday after the ride really backfired. We were both very tired and, beautiful though Northumbria was, we decided to head south. After visiting my sister in Derby, where they had hung out congratulations bunting and prepared a really lovely meal, we returned to Kent and home. We both agreed to return the following year but on a coach tour so that we could enjoy Scotland rather than endure it.

I was very fit physically at the end of the ride which is what I had been told would happen, but I was also tired. I found this a strange phenomenon.

Although I had lost weight and increased muscle tone and improved the cardio-vascular system, I really did not want to cycle any more. This was, I assume, a psychological issue. It was as though my mind was programmed to switch off *the desire to cycle mode* as soon as we reached John O' Groats.

Many people have asked me since if I'll do it again. My unreserved answer has always been, **'Never again'.**

PPS

Perhaps it's a sign that I write almost as slowly as I pedal, when I started this book Lance Armstrong had won five tours – he has now won seven times and retired. He is still free of cancer and may pursue a career in politics. My friend John also completed Land's End to John O' Groats and I have included his riding statistics along with mine just to show what a real cyclist can do.

Carolyn did complete her theology diploma and has been accepted for training as a priest in the Anglican Church, which will include studying towards a Bachelor of Arts Degree.

We did revisit most of our Scottish journey one year later going all the way to John O' Groats on a coach tour. We really soaked up the spectacular scenery and beauty of that land.

NOTES

Day 1: *Lands End - 'we couldn't wait to leave'*

Day 1: *Lunch stop at St Ives: 'a beautiful Cornish seaside town'*

Day 3: *'Much better ride today, crossed the border into Devon'*

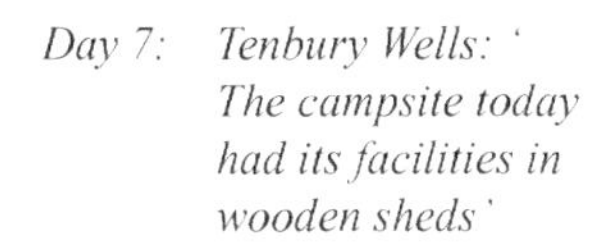

Day 7: *Tenbury Wells: ' The campsite today had its facilities in wooden sheds'*

Day 9: 'Richard rode well, it was good to have his company'

Day 12: The start of the Kirkstone Pass - 'definitely 2 lumps of Kendal Mint Cake'

Day 12: Top of the Kirkstone Pass - 'punched the air if only with one hand'

Day 12: 'A lovely ride past Ullswater brought me to Pooley Bridge'

Day 13: 'Crossing the border today - a major psychological boost - I can't believe I've got this far'

Day 16: Rannock Moor described by R L Stevenson in Kidnapped *'as waste as the sea'*

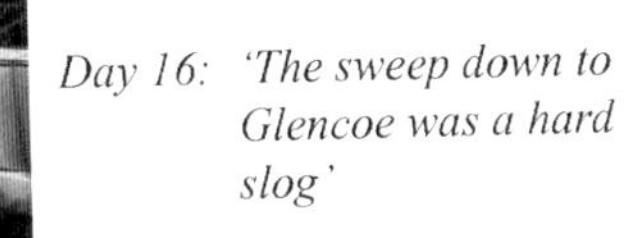

Day 16: 'The sweep down to Glencoe was a hard slog'

Day 18: 'Today I saw the first signpost with John O' Groats on it since leaving Lands End'

Day 18: On the bank of Cromarty Firth 'I could taste the salt air and smell the whisky'

Day 20: 'But the greatest feeling was seeing Orkney Islands from the top of Wrath Hill in Caithness'

Day 20: 'It was as though my mind was programmed to switch off the desire to cycle mode as soon as we reached John O' Groats'

'Many people have asked me since if I'll do it again, my unreserved answer has always been never again!

Log of The Ride

I wrote up my log at the end of each day and although I did make some corrections after the ride, I hope it does capture a little of what happened, as it happened, on the journey.

Thursday 5th June 2003

Up at 5.30 a.m. left home at 6 a.m. Stopped after 100 miles for breakfast. Weather sunny. At 12.30 p.m. today I was playing with my mobile phone and discovered my first text message from Emma & Richard – Happy cycling, lots of love. I replied, I think! I hadn't had a mobile phone since leaving B.T. some years ago, but was persuaded to carry one by my family, how sad is that!

Day 1

Friday 6th June   Land's End to St.Agnes

Woke to thick mist and heavy rain on the campsite at St.Agnes.

Felt very apprehensive about the whole thing.

Arrived at Land's End 10 a.m. Really tacky place. You pay £3 to park in a puddle and then they tell you that you can't stand next to the signpost pointing to John O'Groats without paying another £5 to take photos. Well we did take some pictures and no we didn't give them £5.

We stood far enough from the sign post to be outside the exclusion zone and used a telephoto lens …sorry about that Peter D'Savory, the millionaire who owns Land's End, hope you didn't mind. We couldn't wait to leave!

Lovely ride along B roads back to St Agnes via St Ives, Portreath and Porthtowan. Lots of bluebells, cow parsley and wild foxgloves. Lovely to hear cuckoos and see and hear skylarks. Lunch stop at St Ives, a beautiful Cornish seaside town.

Very hilly route, needed all the gears.

The road along the coast is spectacular: B3306 – B3301 – B3300

Stats: Weather: cloud, rain, mist and sun
Wind, from south-west moderate
Duration 4 .5 hours
Distance 42 miles
Average speed 11.5 mph
Max speed 35.5 mph

Day 2

Saturday 7th June St Agnes to Camelford

Got lost day – could not find correct road out of St Columb Major and ended up on the A30. Unless the earth had changed its orbit, I was also heading towards the sun and not going away from it, i.e. southern bearing instead of north.

All the signposts seemed to point to a place called St Austell – I'm sure it's very nice there but I did not want to go there and it did not feature on my map.

However, I went round the largest wind power plant in Cornwall, twice!

And eventually with the help of my compass and a friendly local cyclist I retraced my route and picked up the northerly heading past the Cornwall show ground on the A39 or Atlantic Highway as it is known.

There is a problem with friendly local cyclists who say 'follow me I'll get you back on the right road'. I have this trouble when I bump into Johnny Barnes. In case you don't know he is a real cyclist and is the husband of the Vicar of Longfield. You see they pedal at a rate with which I am not familiar. I managed to hang on to his wheel until he pointed me in the right direction, I hope he didn't think me rude when he said goodbye but I was not in any state to say anything remotely coherent!

I can imagine what he said when he got home that night 'do you know who I met today, some old geezer, lost on Bodmin Moor, who thinks he's going to cycle to John O' Groats … chortle chortle'.

Used both bottles of drink today!

Stats: Weather: dry/cloudy
Wind, from south-west
Duration 6 hours
Distance 60 miles
Average speed 11.9 mph
Max speed 38 mph

Day 3

Sunday 8th June Camelford to Okehampton

We camped on a pretty grotty site. There were rodent droppings amongst other delights in what was described as the shower block.

We had the company of a wind farm next to us. A strange whoosh whoosh sound sent us into a deep sleep that night, or were we just knackered!

Went to Church in Camelford – the Vicar was a cyclist, he was of course a very nice man!

Legs felt a bit leaded at start but soon loosened up. Much better ride today.

Crossed border into Devon. Very steep hill up to castle at Launceston.

Never really warmed up today. The wind was just right, like a light hand on back – but odd rain shower cooled things down and the sun never emerged.

Lovely rolling countryside. Good stop for sandwich/Kendal mint cake and dried fruit – only used half the drink supply today

Stats: Weather: odd rain shower, no sun
Wind, south-west light
Duration 4 hours
Distance 37 miles
Average speed 12 mph
Max speed 36 mph

Day 4

Monday 9th June Okehampton to Wellington

A good day's riding – rolling countryside with some steep hills especially the one out of Bradninch.

Got a bit lost towards the end. Found a man in garage putting a new cylinder head gasket on a Land Rover – he pointed me in the right direction by saying 'go out of here and turn right' while pointing left – his accent or is it a dialect was so broad I couldn't really understand him anyway, shame he couldn't speak English!

A rare sighting on a country lane – insulators No.1, I think, ceramic, white – loads of them on an O.H. (overhead) telephone supply.

I worked on those when I was an apprentice and trained on the O.H. at the Sydenham training school on poles that were 6 foot tall.

I noticed that the soil colour changed to red in Devon – this wasn't because I had cut my knee or had a U.T.I. If you don't know what that is, don't bother asking.

A special treat today was that Carolyn had sussed out a swimming pool in Wellington – it was a really good 30m pool.

Courtesy of Dr Andrew from the Ellenor, I am reading *French Revolutions* – the story of a man and his dream to cycle the route of the Tour de France. The author talks about the speed and endurance of the pro cyclist on such a tour. On average they do about 2,300 miles over 16 mountains in 3 weeks and reached speeds of over 60 mph.

It is no surprise that if they were to hold a senior's event, they might have trouble getting a quorum!

Stats: Weather: mainly cloud and cool
Wind, from the west
Duration 4 .25 hours
Distance 48 miles
Average speed 11 mph
Max speed 43 mph …which was really stupid

Day 5

Tuesday 10th June Wellington to Bath

A noisy journey today – not alas the sound of bird song or rippling stream, although the excellent camp site in Bath provided that.

The noise of cars/lorries. Most of the ride was on A roads and first half mainly flat and across the Somerset levels. Meopham has a few rumble strips designed to slow down the traffic – Somerset has the A361 and it runs for 10 miles – perhaps the Romans built it and nobody has been back since to maintain it.

Today I climbed the Mendips. The ride book describes it as a serious climb. However I couldn't help noticing a sign halfway up 'Duck Eggs' – I did! The final insult towards the top of the 3-mile climb – just before the peak at 800ft, was a sign on the road – 'Slow' – I didn't – if I had, I would have fallen off!

Stats: Weather: sun/cloud
Wind, west/south-west
Duration 5.5 hours
Distance 55 miles
Average speed 13.3 mph
Max speed 35.5 mph

Post Script.
I heard on our return to Kent, that Alan & Myrtle Rogers, who was the former minister at the Baptist Church in Meopham, had seen me on the climb out of Wells.

Day 6

Wednesday 11th June Bath to Newent

Started off with a cycling companion. Carolyn came along the canal towpath to Bath, for just over 2 miles, on the Moulton bike. We had a hot chocolate in the Salvation Army centre in Bath.

Found Bath rather cycle un-friendly to get out of: solid traffic jams, poor road signing and no cycle ways or even the merest hint of a concession to pedal power. Long climb out of Bath on A46. I should have taken the B road route – but could not find it. The A46 from Bath to the M4 is like a rat run for 38 ton 24 wheel lorries and I felt like a little mouse. When the lorries overtake you on single carriageway at 60 mph I think James Dyson or Edgar Hoover, was it he or his brother – they both suck anyway, would be mightily impressed: the words vacuum and vortex come to mind as they suck you into a near death encounter. It was a frightening experience. However, after crossing the M4 the road became eerily quiet and I could catch glimpses of Wales across the Severn valley. Fitness is proving to be OK, but the dreaded saddle soreness arrived today. Let's hope the Savlon works.

It was really good to spend last evening with friends from our pre-married days, Mike and Jill Adams whom we have not seen for over 30 years. He looks a bit like Patrick Moore, but has a serious spinal problem and is quite confined physically. They gave us a simple but wholesome meal and Carolyn acquired a couple of theological books for her studies. We heard all about their family and how their sons were getting on. They seemed to have better memories than I do. They were telling me things about me that I had forgotten. Fortunately most of it was OK! Looking forward to watching the England-Slovakia game tonight on our 4" BW TV. We can just get a picture here.

Stats: Weather: lovely summer day
Wind, light breeze from S/SW
Duration 5 hours
Distance 55 mph
Average speed 11.8 mph
Max speed 32 mph

Day 7

Thursday 12th June   Newent to Tenbury Wells

A day for crossing county boundaries. In and out of Gloucestershire, Herefordshire, Shropshire and Worcestershire. I'm not sure which one I'm in at the end of the day but we are in the village of Orleton.

Ledbury is an impressive looking town. Apparently mentioned in the Doomsday Book. I like the way my route guide describes the two-mile climb out of Bromyard as moderate, it seemed somewhat more than that. Perhaps the wind was blowing the wrong way today. The saddle soreness of yesterday is no worse – I hope I don't become Savlon intolerant – it seems to be working – at least for the present.

The countryside became more forested today and less wild. The roads were good and traffic mainly light.

A first today – I overtook two cyclists on the hill up from Tenbury Wells - they were carrying all their luggage and both had double panniers.

The campsite today has its facilities in wooden sheds – but everything works and we had the site to ourselves. A lovely old Pub in the village where we had great food.

Stats: Weather: warm to hot sun
Wind, light breeze
Duration 4 hours
Distance 41 miles
Average speed 12.5 mph
Max speed 31.5 mph

Day 8

Friday 13th June Tenbury Wells to Shrewsbury

I had an 8 a.m. call from John Barnes of Longfield – he realised that today I would be cycling through Church Stretton and said that he and Katrina had visited the town on their bikes last year and had a good cup of tea in a café. Well, I'm afraid John that all the cafés I looked in were far too posh for me and my Lycra – must have been Katrina's charm that got you in!

The forecast was for a hot day and it was certainly the hottest day of the tour yet. The B roads were often under a canopy of trees so gave some welcome shade. The flora and fauna seemed similar to Kent.

No significant climbs today. I watched a four ball drive off on the Ludlow Golf Course – which is situated within the running track, if that's what it is called, of Ludlow Race Course. I thought to myself that is what I would be doing today if I wasn't riding from Land's End to John O'Groats. I usually play on Friday mornings which is my day off.

Quite a lot of today's ride was on the old Roman road called Watling Street. Several fords cross the road – one of them was still flowing.

The heat was a significant factor and will take some getting used to if it continues. The end of the ride was around the outskirts of Shrewsbury and although very cycle friendly, with off-road cycle routes, was very noisy. The campsite is the most luxurious yet, booked especially for our guests due to arrive later. Although I was using sun block on my face and arms, the backs of my legs did get burnt. Because I am travelling mainly due north the sun is nearly always behind me. I must remember that for other days if the sun continues to shine. What a Wally!

Stats: Weather: hot – mostly unbroken sun
Wind, light, variable
Duration 5 hours
Distance 47 miles
Average speed 12.3
Max speed 27 mph

Day 9

Saturday 14th June Shrewsbury to Chester

Our eldest daughter Emma, who is pregnant, arrived with her husband last evening. A real joy today was to have Richard, our son-in-law with me on the ride. We hired the campsite swimming pool last evening just for the four of us. It was lovely.

One thing that appealed to my sense of humour was a notice in the swimming pool advising swimmers that if any one urinated in the pool then the person responsible would be liable to pay the cost of draining and refilling the pool. I just wondered how they would manage to work out who the culprit would be if there were 20 or 30 people using it. Another of life's great unexplained mysteries! We were taken to the start of the ride by Emma and Carolyn because we were camped on the wrong side of Shrewsbury. This wasn't cheating on the ride because I had cycled round the ring road the previous day and was just going back to pick up the A458 where I had left it on Friday … surprisingly enough it was still there! The ride book showed that the terrain was mainly flat – but that did not detract from a really pretty journey through stunning country-side.

We were in Wales for about an hour – in fact had our sandwiches in a pub car park in Wales, unfortunately the pub was shut. I drank a toast out of my water bottle to the only Welsh man I could think of … my friend Reg Bain who has been having a bit of a tough time of late. We met another end to end-er today – a man from Derby who is staying in Youth Hostels. He hoped that the hills of Cornwall and Devon were the worst on the ride – I echo that! The last part of our ride today, about 3 miles was from the centre of Chester along the Shropshire Union Canal to our campsite. It was lovely to look over to the West today and see clearly the mountains of Wales profiled against a blue sky.

Stats: Weather: hot,
Wind, negligible
Duration 4 hours
Distance 45 miles
Average speed 13.2mph
Max speed 27mph *Post Script Richard rode really well it was good to have his company.*

Day10

Sunday 15th June Chester to Croston

Left Emma and Richard in the middle of Chester, said our goodbyes. Carolyn and I walked to the Cathedral where we parted company – Carolyn to a service and me to ride into Lancashire. If yesterday's ride was an enjoyable experience, today's ride was mostly a dreary drudge. The early part of the ride was along the Western Express Way – I'm glad it was Sunday at least there weren't too many lorries. Merseyside looked so drear and even smelt pretty gross. The major part of the industry was based on salt brought up from Cheshire in barges. It was the Leblanc process, which turned sodium chloride into soda ash or sodium carbonate, required to make soap and glass.

A lot of the ride went through housing estates and small industrial sites.

I had arranged to meet Carolyn in the car park of Croston railway station, not that Carolyn was particularly happy with that because it meant having to drive 50 miles up the M6 from Chester to find me.

I had originally planned to return to Cheshire with my bike, by train, because we had been invited to spend the evening and night with friends from our Gravesend days, Ruth and Steve Broadfoot in Middlewich. Unfortunately there were no trains running on Sundays! I had a shower in the van whilst parked in the station car park, and a 50-mile drive back down the M6. We went to the evening service with Ruth & Steve at their church. We then had a lovely meal and went to bed at 12.15 a.m.

Stats: Weather: hot & sunny
Wind, negligible
Duration 4 hours
Distance 48 miles
Average speed 13.1mph
Max speed 27mph

Day 11

Monday 16th June Leyland to Milnthorpe

Awoke at 4.30 a.m. – sunlight in window/birds singing. Steve left home at about 6.30 a.m. I didn't hear him singing with the lark which is a shame because he has a good voice. Carolyn had a bath!! It was lovely to see our friends Ruth and Steve and to catch up on all their news.

Today's tour started at Leyland, the same latitude as Croston but I had done that bit yesterday, further along the B5253 so as not to miss out any of the end to end. Carolyn therefore had to drive me back up the M6 about 50 miles and then another 50 miles to Cumbria to find the next campsite! Leyland is famous for its trucks. A local blacksmith, James Sumner, put a lawn mower engine on a tricycle and won first prize at Royal Lancashire Agricultural Show in 1890. In 1896 along with others he produced a steam-powered van, a year later an 18-seater bus with a top speed of 10mph. Within 5 years the petrol engine had replaced steam and the rest is history. I'm still driving my Dad's Austin Allegro built by the now defunct British Leyland Motor Corporation. I do not find it surprising that any company that could design and build the Austin Allegro would not now be defunct! I crossed several canals today, in fact it was probably the same one, no, I didn't get lost!, the tour crossed and re-crossed the Lancaster Canal – designed by John Rennie in 1797. He is best known for building London Bridge, which was sold for £1.5 million and moved to Arizona and re-opened in 1971. Did you know Preston, for whom Tom Finney played gets its name from Priest's Town. Richard Arkwright was born there in 1732, if you don't know who he was, or for that matter, Tom Finney, shame on you! I had a lovely encounter in the middle of Lancaster. A cyclist came up beside me at traffic lights – he was going to John O'Groats – he asked me when I had left Land's End – I said with some pride that it was Friday a week ago. 'When did you leave?' I asked him. 'On Saturday', he said, then raced off. I'm glad I didn't insult him by asking which Saturday. However, the story is not yet told – at the next set of lights, yes, I do stop at them, a van pulled up – and a man said, 'Off to John O'Groats then?' They had Race Against Time charity stickers on the windows – they were the support vehicle for the racer and in radio contact. 'He'll be in Gretna tonight and John O'Groats on Wednesday' he said. That's 5 days end to end – that's 200 miles a day, I thought!! Anyway he was a lot younger than me and looked like a real cyclist!! Found Carolyn on a lovely site in Cumbria – a few miles from Kendal. The ride today was through mainly flat country side but the Pennines were clearly visible to the east and from A6 out of Lancaster I could see Morecambe Bay to the West.

Stats: Weather: cloudless sky.
Wind, what wind!
Duration 4 hours.
Distance 43 miles.
Average speed 14.1mph.
Max speed 25 mph

Day12

Tuesday 17th June Milnthorpe to Ullswater

Heavy rain overnight and it felt like a sauna early on in the ride today. I decided to follow the A roads to Windermere – Steve Broadfoot's helpful advice about the traffic on some main roads proved really helpful. There was a cycle track along the A59. It was fine.

The first big climb for several days towards Windermere was testing, but conscious of The Kirkstone Pass to come, I took it easy.

It was lovely to see Lake Windermere suddenly appear between the hills. It's England's largest lake. I didn't go into Windermere town but headed for the start of The Pass. I remember the Vicar at Darenth used to advise his congregation if the sermon was one or two mints long. I have decided that Judith's one lump of Kendal Mint Cake, which has sustained me daily, would have to be doubled today. So a 2 mint hill. This was the toughest climb of the whole tour – a 1300 foot gain in elevation over 6 miles – and is the highest mountain pass in England. It was a very tough climb – but I made it without stopping and had my break at the top. The tour then went down the other side – dominated by Helvellyn to the west – at 3118 feet it is second highest peak in England. A lovely ride past Brothers Water and about 10 miles along Ullswater brought me to Pooley Bridge where Carolyn had parked up on a campsite on the edge of Ullswater. We went on a cruise for about an hour on the lake in the evening. Carolyn got severely midged today. I think we are about half way in miles to John O' Groats. I feel very tired after today's ride.

Stats: Weather: steamy early, fresh later
Wind, negligible
Duration 4 hours
Distance 45 miles
Average speed 11.4mph
Max speed 30mph

Day 13

Wednesday 18th June Ullswater to Dumfries

The planned ride was 61 miles but it was 5 miles up a severe hill out of Ullswater to get to the start point. The weather was poor but for the ride up to Carlisle the wind was not really a factor – leafy lanes well sheltered. Crossed the border today, a major psychological boost, looked around Gretna, still can't really believe I've got this far.

Welcome to Scotland.

As the ride moved into Scotland and certainly on the stretch from Gretna to Dumfries, which was almost due west, the wind was a major factor. The Solway Firth looks wonderful, but with very little protection from the Westerly gales, my legs really hurt. We had arranged to meet at the Burns Centre in Dumfries because Carolyn had found what looked in the book to be a really good camp site about 10 miles west of Dumfries and I did not fancy another 10 miles.I eventually found Carolyn and the camper having spotted her across the River Nith. Famous though Robbie Burns is within Dumfries, he died here in 1796, we both found the signs for the Robert Burns Centre almost non-existent. Signs for the other Robert Burns places of fame were easy to find, but they were not the places we agreed to meet up. So extra miles at the start and twice round Dumfries at the end took me up to 70 miles. Hopefully the longest ride of the tour!! The site really was great – with indoor heated pool/sauna/excellent restaurant and views over a loch.

Stats: Weather: wet/damp
Wind, gale force westerly
Duration 5.5 hours
Distance 69 miles
Average speed 12.7 mph
Max speed 31mph

Day 14

Thursday 19th June   Dumfries to Drongon

I could see the rain coming across the mountains from the West. I was about 30 miles out when it hit me. The temperature dropped and I got really cold. In one little village there was an Indian take-away – so I asked for a takeaway Indian tea – 'solly, no do tea'. I think they might have, but I guess she did not want me standing on her clean take-away floor dripping water. However a garage nearby did hot drinks – so cold was I that the lady offered to operate the serve yourself machine for me. The wind today was really serious – mostly coming over my left shoulder – but the gusts were severe and dangerous. On a better day it would have been a really good ride. Most of the tour was through pine forests – which accounted for most of the traffic: lorries loaded with timber – the smell of pine filled the air. Thanks to some local information from someone at last night's stop-over I kept mainly on A roads – which were fine. The A712 and A713 – so navigation today was really easy. For the first time I arrived at a campsite before Carolyn. I was not surprised she didn't want to leave our previous site. Today's site was a bit Butlins-like with a ghastly reception area accessed through smoke-filled corridors, just what I needed after cycling over 50 miles! I did have a swim to freshen up and warm up however. We are just 4 miles from Ayr and had a text message from our friends, Patricia and Michael Jupp that they were heading for the Trossachs so we might arrange a rendezvous. We ventured out to the coast at Ayr and should have been able to see the Isle of Arran. The weather was dreadful but I did get out of the van and asked the one person I bumped into if that shadow in the mist and rain out west was Arran; she said it was. As a family we spent a lovely holiday on the island when the children were young. We went further up the coast so that I could see Royal Troon Golf Course where the Open Championship is sometimes played. The wind was so strong it was barely possible to stand up, how people can play golf in conditions like that I cannot imagine.

Stats: Weather: heavy rain for last half of ride
Wind, severe westerly gusts
Duration 5 hours
Distance 55 miles
Average speed 12 mph
Max speed 35 mph

Day15

Friday 20th June Drongon to Balloch

Wind, rain, mist, wind, ferrets, kestrels, wind, herons, skylarks, hydroelectric power station, dams, wind. These are the words that come to mind as I write up today's ride. Started the ride today at Drongan. The wind was still a factor and the forecast gave little sign of relief – rain was also about. Seemed like hard work for the first 20 or 25 miles – climbing to about 700 feet through lovely countryside mainly agricultural livestock. The ride went close to Dreghorn – birthplace of John Dunlop the inventor of the pneumatic bicycle tyre. No, I still haven't had a puncture, although John Barnes phoned me yesterday to say he had two in a day coming home from work and had to walk. Life's just not fair sometimes! The journey through Paisley was not the most heightened cultural experience of the tour. Did you know that it was because of the terrible conditions in the weaving mills of Glasgow and Paisley in the early 1800s in the so-called sweatshops that we still call our pullovers sweaters! It reminded me a bit of the worst parts of Vauxhall/Old Kent Road and Bermondsey.

On approaching the Erskine Bridge notices said the road was closed and a diversion along the A8 was offered. I asked a workman if bikes could get through. What a shame, I had not brought my Scottish phrase book so I went on anyway and carried my bike over piles of building materials – I don't think the shouts I heard were directed at me!

A longish climb up from the toll bridge that crosses the Clyde, which is free for cyclists, brought me to Balloch, where we arranged to stay over. After a shower, mug of tea and flapjack, I wandered round the campsite, which was a most attractive looking place, and discovered a leisure suite. So booked it for an hour. It was lovely – two of us in a great big Jacuzzi and a sauna, loungers etc. in a pine cabin. Then Patricia and Michael arrived – they were staying about 20 miles away. It was a really good evening – we ate out in a small local café and they treated us! It was really good to see our old friends so far from home.

Stats: Weather: part rain/ mist part dry/cloudy
Wind, strong westerly
Duration 5 hours
Distance 57 miles
Average speed 12.4 mph
Max speed 34 mph

Day16

Saturday 21st June Balloch to Glencoe

I was still running with the idea of trying to reduce the ride from 21 days to 20 days by doing some extra miles for a few days. The excellent guidebook planned the ride over 21 days but I had thought that if my fitness was OK then I could do some extra miles in Scotland and compress the time. So today was one to have a go. The objective was to get to Glencoe – about 70 miles. The first part of the ride – about 25 miles, was pretty flat following the banks of Loch Lomond. The next 35 were very demanding, climbing through from the Lowlands to the Highlands. One of the climbs, to Rannoch Moor, which is described by Robert Louis Stevenson in Kidnapped as being 'as waste as the sea', is especially severe. I saw several deer – unfortunately all dead – I assume hit by vehicles. The forecast was for rain, but I only got wet when I entered the clouds at about 800 feet. There were lots of walkers about doing a highland trek for charity and I encountered about 20 cyclists on a ride ending up in Edinburgh. They were very friendly – one of them even stopped and took a picture for me. The wind today was still westerly so the sweep down through the glen to Glencoe, which should have been a free wheel, was a hard slog. But the dramatic backdrop of the mountains made it worthwhile. It was lovely to see Mel & Leslie Green and their young children, Joshua and Rosie, friends from our days in Gravesend, before we set off. They live in Balloch and seem very happy, but it must be a difficult life when Leslie has to go away for 3 months at a time in his boat – his words. Actually it's a nuclear submarine and he is a Lieutenant on board. Mel says she has a good group of friends around her and the children were wonderful.

Back to the ride – the midges are a real problem. At Glencoe people are walking about in midge nets. We are trying candle burning in the van. Carolyn is more vulnerable than me at present and has a lot of bites. They obviously only bite sweet people! My own fitness is fine – I am glad that I took sound advice and restricted the early days to 40/50 miles. Although 70 miles a day is now OK I'm pretty sure I could not have sustained that throughout. Carolyn set out on the Moulton to find me today by cycling south on the A82. However, I took the alternative minor road into Glencoe about 4 miles back – it was a lovely thought though.
We heard via a text message that James, our oldest grandchild aged 6 had been injured playing in his first football tournament in Dartford. Apparently not a career threatening problem, so he'll be back to play another day.

Stats: Weather: mainly dry, wet in mountain, mist & cold
Wind, strong westerly
Duration 6 hours
Distance 69 miles
Average speed 13.7 mph
Max speed 28 mph

Day17

Sunday 22nd June Glencoe to Drumnadrochit

A real Scottish Highland Baptism – wind – rain – even some thunder and lightning. We went to the little Scottish Episcopal Church in Glencoe – we walked in the rain – Carolyn got very wet, well it's only a little umbrella!. I think us walking into the Church lowered the average age by about 20 years. I am still trying to understand what it was all about. The organist obviously wanted to play Scottish reels rather than some pretty drab hymns. The priest seemed to be on some sort of autopilot – totally oblivious of his congregation. His sermon had no point whatsoever and the communion wine was obviously from Del Boy in Only Fools and Horses when he bought 20 cases of communion wine only to discover it was white wine! The day could only get better – or could it? We got wet coming back from church. My ride was a planned 65/70 miles to complete my aim to finish on Wednesday. I did not however reckon on the weather. It was simply awful. Only about 15 miles not in the rain and during that part I got my first puncture of the ride. It could have been a lot worse – I saw the pothole on a descent, but could not avoid it because cars were overtaking at the time. The front wheel hit it hard and the inner tube blew and although I managed to stay on the bike, I thought the wheel would be damaged, but got away with just the puncture. I had my sandwiches by Loch Lochy in the dry period. The scenery was simply stunning. Although Ben Nevis was clear to the peak at 4410ft when I cycled through Fort William, storm clouds were gathering. The wind was constantly head on but thankfully not too strong. My legs were tired after yesterday and this ride was a real battle especially when the rain started again and made the earlier downpour seem like a shower! I was very grateful to arrive in Drumnadrochit and have a hot shower, big mug of hot tea and later haggis and chips, if that's not irreverent to any Scot reading this. We stayed on a site at a farm with mixed cattle and an equestrian centre perched on a hill a few hundred feet above Loch Ness.

Stats: Weather: rain from heavy to ow this hurts it's so hard!
Wind, constant moderate northerly, head on.
Duration 6 hours
Distance 68 miles
Average speed 13.5 mph
Max speed 24 mph

Post Script We have since discovered that Del Boy has sold lots of white wine to the Anglican Church as well, down as far as Kent. I'm not sure what the theological issues are but it would seem to be common practice. Answers on a post card to the author please.
On our return journey some days later, in the camper van, I showed Carolyn where I hit the pothole. Guess what, there was a splodge of fresh tarmac where they had filled it in!

Day18

Monday 23rd June Drumnadrochit to Tain

After the drenching yesterday I did some maintenance on the bike, and checked the spare inner tube just in case I had another puncture. A really lovely ride apart from the first and last 5 miles! Most of the tour today was along the banks of the Cromarty Firth and crossing it twice because I misread the map. Carolyn passed me on the southern bank of the Firth just by the bridge; she had travelled up via Inverness and visited the shops. This was the first time our paths have crossed. At one part of the ride around Invergordon I could taste the salt from sea air and smell the local whisky distillery. If I was a sailor I might have thought I'd died and woken up in heaven. Invergordon is also a base for the construction and repair of North Sea oilrigs. There were several out in the Firth. Approaching Tain the smell of the Glenmorangie distillery was evident. This brand is the third most popular malt brand in the world. It seemed almost a shame that I don't actually like the stuff! The start of today's ride brought another first. The guide describes the first three miles as a tough ride. I am beginning to get a feel for the language of the author. He uses words like steep, gradual, and tough to describe hills. For me, 'tough' meant unclimbable. I was resolute in my mind that with the gearing I had on the bike I could climb any hill – but my lungs/knees/thighs had other ideas. I'm not sure which gave out first, but the other two soon came out in sympathy. As for my resolute mind well, I gave all that I had but it wasn't enough. So my first walk up a hill. My left knee was very painful from yesterday's ride and although cycling gave little pain, walking up that hill was very painful. The last few miles from Tain to the campsite at Dornoch Bridge was on a westerly heading across open farmland into a westerly gale! It was a real battle to keep going. Today I saw the first sign post with John O' Groats on it. The first time I've seen the place name since Land's End. The end is nigh! In the evening it was good to have a chat with John Barnes again.

He is a great encouragement. We went to bed about 11 p.m. and it was still light!

Stats: Weather: occcasional sun, no rain
Wind, strong westerly
Duration 4.5 hours
Distance 55 miles
Average speed 13.3 mph
Max speed 33 mph

Day19

Tuesday 24th June Tain to Dunbeath

We planned a rendezvous at Golspie – about 15 miles from Dornoch. This was very nice – we had a stroll along the sea front and then a drink in a really pleasant little café. Carolyn then set off to find the night's stopover at Dunbeath and I continued pedalling. It was a lovely ride, mainly along the cliff tops with the North Sea for company.

It was a hilly day, over 1000 feet of climbing in two climbs. I felt as though I was on reserve tank today, but managed the climbs.

I saw sheep shearing on a farm and some of the famous highland cattle – fearsome-looking beasts with woolly coats and horns and hardy enough to stay out over winter and survive on the slim pickings of Highland shrubs and gorse. I met a lady on the road doing end to end. She was travelling solo on an aged Raleigh mountain bike and had left Land's End 4 days before me. I said I would see her at John O' Groats tomorrow. The oilrigs are clearly visible from Dunbeath. Neil Gunn, a writer, was born in Dunbeath and a memorial is featured in the village – I've not heard of him but must investigate further – he sounds a bit like a Scottish Hemmingway. A very friendly, albeit basic campsite provided us with our penultimate overnight stay of the ride. The local rhubarb was in abundance and happy campers were asked to help themselves – which we did. The owner of the site, who came here from Kent 3 years ago, said that the castle, prominent on the cliff-top overlooking the harbour at Dunbeath, is owned by the Avery Corporation of America. The castle, which is 17th Century, was involved in a plot to restore Charles 1st to the throne. However, the Marquis of Montrose, who was the King's defender in Scotland, was defeated in the battle of Dornoch

Firth. He was captured and executed in Edinburgh. I heard and saw curlews today, they have very distinctive hooked bills. Next to the campsite were two telephone exchange buildings, almost identical in size. One of the buildings was empty but I could see enough to work out that it was, once upon a time a U.A.X. (unit automatic exchange) and similar to ones I looked after in the 1960s in wild parts of Kent. The other building contained modern digital kit, about which I know nothing! We walked down to the little harbour and found a fishing boat called Margaret Ellen the name of my auntie who died earlier this year.

Stats: Weather: dry & sunny.
Wind, negligible
Duration 5 hours.
Distance 49 miles
Average speed 12.6mph
Max speed 34.5mph

Post Script We tried to buy a second hand Neil Gunn book in a Thurso bookshop, but were told that they were quickly snapped up by the locals because of the author's connection with those parts. However in my local library in Meopham they had a copy of Morning Tide by Neil M. Gunn, a story set among the crofters and fisherman of Caithness around the early 20th century and first published in 1930. Isn't it a small world!

Day 20

Wednesday 25th June Dunbeath to John O' Groats

About 40 miles to go – this was the best day in Scotland for weather – the forecast was for fine weather and the whole day was almost cloudless. The ride to J of G was really pleasant – hardly a car on the road but for the first 10 miles my legs felt like lead. Stopped in Wick – spotted the camper-van in Safeway's car park. Couldn't see Carolyn so left her a note. It was a beautiful sight at the top of Wrath Hill looking down on J of G and today seeing clearly the Orkney Isles. Carolyn, who had overtaken me earlier, was on the roadside to cheer me home and I met the lady I saw yesterday, the one on the old mountain bike, who was from Wales. She was returning to Wick to get the train to Aberdeen to visit her son. We congratulated each other. Carolyn texted all the friends and family in the support group at home – and every one of them texted back – brilliant! We went to Thurso in the afternoon. What a lovely seaside town – we found the place where Sir William Smith the Founder of the Boys' Brigade was born – in a farm building on the outskirts of the town. We then celebrated with a meal in a Chinese restaurant. We sent 68 postcards to friends who had sponsored us.

Stats: Weather: brilliant, sun
Wind, westerly light
Duration 2.5 hours
Distance 38 miles
Average speed 14.4mph
Max speed 30.5 mph

Overall Statistics

(my friend John's in brackets...but he is a real cyclist!)

Total Distance Cycled:	1025 miles	(1018 miles… he had satellite navigation!)
Average speed:	12.6 m.p.h.	(17.4 m.p.h.)
Highest Speed:	43 m.p.h.	(49 m.p.h.)
Time spent in saddle:	94 hours	(59 hours 24 minutes,..no wonder he didn't get saddle sore)
Duration:	20 Days: 4 with rain	(11 Days)

One puncture: no mechanical breakdowns;

Carolyn drove 2600 miles in camper van:

Appendix 1

Maslow's Hierarchy of Needs

Maslow's thesis is that the human being develops in a sequence, not haphazardly, and that only as he is able to satisfy the lower needs can he move up through the others.

Aesthetic Needs

Looking for reasons, truth, symmetry, beauty, justice and appreciating a vision of greatness.

Cognitive Needs

Need to know and understand the world. Curiosity to tackle the unknown.

Need for Self-Actualisation

Achieving one's full potential. Realising self-fulfilment. Seeking to become what you are capable of becoming. Seeking self-awareness.

Need for Esteem and Status

Need for self-respect and respect from others, sense of achievement, reputation, prestige and success.

Love and Belongingness Needs

Identification with others. Need for affection and acceptance. Relating to others, first to parents and siblings. Need to love and to be loved.

Biological Needs

Food. Drink. Sleep. Warmth. Shelter. Freedom from pain. Sex.

For the people of faith, maybe, the base line might be:

Seek ye first the Kingdom of God.

Appendix 2

The Bike

Trek 1200: Aluminium frame

9-speed cassette range 11-32 teeth on sprockets

Triple front chain set using 52-42-30 teeth on sprockets

Weight: 22lbs unladen

Appendix 3

The total amount collected including Gift Aid was £6479.77

This was divided as directed by the sponsors in the following proportions:

Cancer Research U.K.	£ 1556.97
Ellenor Foundation	£ 1665.19
S.C.C.S.	£ 1922.61
St.John's, Meopham	£ 1335.00

Thanks to all the sponsors